God is forever reaching into the maelstrom of the death culture and holding out His hand. The following pages tell the real-life story of one who kept taking hold of His hand — an authentic and engaging witness to the transforming power of a "yes" to God. This is a "must read" for youth, parents, teachers, and ministers at every level. Respond to the invitation to breathe in deeply this dawn of the new evangelization! Thank you, Mary-Louise!

— GREG SCHLUETER
DIRECTOR OF THE DIOCESAN OFFICE OF YOUTH AND YOUNG
ADULT MINISTRY, ERIE, PENNSYLVANIA
MAGNIFICAT! MINISTRIES

We may disagree, but Mary-Louise Kurey stands with courage both on *Politically Incorrect* and in the pages of this book.

— BILL MAHER
HOST OF ABC's *POLITICALLY INCORRECT*

An inspiring testimonial with sound research that is sure to speak to young people about the important decisions they face on a daily basis. Kudos to Kurey for her commitment to chastity and for presenting teens with a hopeful alternative to mainstream values.

— THERESE J. BORCHARD
AUTHOR OF *WINGING IT: MEDITATIONS OF A YOUNG ADULT*

This is an engagingly personal story that will keep you turning the pages. Mary-Louise Kurey describes what seemed to her a "mission impossible": persuading a sex-crazed world that true love means saving the beautiful gift of our sexuality for the person who commits to loving us for a lifetime. Her inspiring message is for everyone: God has a unique mission for each one of us, a way He has chosen for us to make a difference in the world. Trust Him, Mary-Louise says; open yourself to Him; let Him make you a rebel for the truth of chastity — and you will live a life without regrets and attain the happiness that every heart longs for. Chastity, her book makes clear, is not a bore or a burden but a journey of joyful love.

— DR. THOMAS LICKONA
AUTHOR OF *EDUCATING FOR CHARACTER: HOW OUR SCHOOLS
CAN TEACH RESPECT AND RESPONSIBILITY*

This girl has guts! Mary-Louise Kurey put her role as Miss Wisconsin at the service of God, and in the process brought the light of chastity to some pretty unlikely — and amazing — places. Once you've read her story, you'll see why she is the perfect role model for "standing with courage."

— MARY BETH BONACCI
NATIONAL CHASTITY SPEAKER; AUTHOR OF *REAL LOVE* AND
WE'RE ON A MISSION FROM GOD

Fresh statement of how one's personal strength, attitude, and courage carve a path to positive decision-making — the foundation for a successful life.

— MELVIN MURPHY
AUTHOR OF *BARBERSHOP TALK* AND *IT'S WHO YOU KNOW*

STANDING WITH
COURAGE
Confronting Tough Decisions About Sex

STANDING WITH COURAGE

Confronting Tough Decisions About Sex

Mary-Louise Kurey,
Miss Wisconsin 1999

OUR SUNDAY VISITOR PUBLISHING DIVISION

OUR SUNDAY VISITOR, INC.

HUNTINGTON, INDIANA 46750

The Scripture citations used in this work are taken from the *Holy Bible, Revised Standard Version, Catholic Edition*, copyright © 1965 and 1966 by the Division of Christian Education of the National Council of the Churches of Christ in the U.S.A., and are used by permission of the copyright holder; all rights reserved. The author and publisher are grateful to those publishers and others (particularly those mentioned in Chapter 6) whose materials, whether in the public domain or protected by copyright laws, have been used in this volume (verbatim or adapted). Special thanks go to Shawnee Press, Inc., for the use of "Walk a Little Slower, My Friend," by Don Besig and Nancy Price, copyright © 1985 by Shawnee Press, Inc. (ASCAP), international copyright secured, all rights reserved, reprinted by permission. Every reasonable effort has been made to determine copyright holders of excerpted materials and to secure permissions as needed. If any copyrighted materials have been inadvertently used in this work without proper credit being given in one form or another, please notify Our Sunday Visitor in writing so that future printings of this work may be corrected accordingly.

Our Sunday Visitor Publishing Division
Our Sunday Visitor, Inc.
200 Noll Plaza
Huntington, IN 46750

ISBN: 1-931709-03-3 (Inventory No. T7)
LCCCN: 2001135284

Cover design by Monica Haneline
Interior design by Sherri L. Hoffman

Cover photo courtesy of AP/Wide World Photos (Mary-Louise Kurey of Brookfield, Miss Wisconsin, talks to a crowd of about one thousand people on Saturday, May 13, 2000, at an anti-abortion rally on the steps of the state capitol of Madison, Wisconsin)

PRINTED IN THE UNITED STATES OF AMERICA

For Mom and Dad,
whose unconditional love gave me
the strength I needed to persevere;

and for Nana,
who believed in my dreams before I did.

Contents

Color Photo Section Included!

Acknowledgments

This book wouldn't be possible without tremendous support from my family and friends. Mom, thanks for all of your guidance and insights, from the conceptualization of this book to its final revisions. Dad, thanks for handling my "gigs" so joyfully and competently, and for always keeping me focused on the task at hand. Nana, thanks for being the best grandmother in the world! I love you so much! Tom and Kim, thank you so much for your love, generosity, and encouragement — and for the laptop computer! (I wrote this book on it!) Kim, I appreciate your edits and great marketing help. John, thank you for being both a terrific brother and mentor to me, for all of your love, and for giving me a wonderful place to live, write, and practice. I never could have done this without you! Elizabeth and David, thanks for believing in me and always encouraging me with lots of love, great advice, and plenty of humor! You are all so special to me.

I'm indebted to all of the wonderful people at Our Sunday Visitor who have worked so hard to make this book the best it can be, especially Michael Dubruiel — your enthusiasm and confidence in me from the very beginning inspired me to put my fears aside and give my all to this book every day. Thank you so much. I also wish to thank Greg Erlandson for being so kind to me, and for caring so much about a first-time author's work. Many thanks to Jill Kurtz for putting your heart into sharing this book with the world — you're awesome and brilliant! Thank you also to Henry O'Brien for your hard work, and to the entire team at OSV.

I'm blessed with many terrific friends whose frank opinions helped me tremendously in shaping this book. An enormous thank-you to Christian Stepansky — you are such a blessing in my life! Thank you for all of the "wonder-filling" work you put into editing this book — and for the joy you bring to my life each day! Heartfelt thanks also to Father Michael Klos, Melvin Murphy, and Rick Celik — your insights and your friendship are priceless.

I also wish to thank some very special people who have touched my life in a beautiful and profound way. To Elayne Bennett — you are my role model, my ideal, the woman I want to be like — thank you for everything you've done for me. Jeff Cavins, your friendship and your ministry are such a treasure in my life! I'm your number one fan! I can't thank you enough! Many thanks also to Deal Hudson, Sam Horn, Kathleen Sullivan, Annie Miller, Art McMaster, and Ed Barrett — your guidance, assistance, friendship, and advice have broadened my horizons and deeply enriched my life and my work.

I also would like to thank all of the wonderful people in the Miss Wisconsin family — especially Sue and Lou Captain — for your friendship, enthusiasm, and support of my work. Thanks also to Doug Black and Monica Shipley for always believing in me, and for your invaluable help on my long journey to the crown. Without you, none of this would have been possible. Many thanks to Marilyn Runge and Cheryl Gotts from Milwaukee Best Friends for believing in me from the beginning and for the many opportunities you've given me. A great big thank-you to all of the teens and young adults whom I've met through this work over the years. Your enthusiasm for chastity and your sincere stories have touched my heart. Finally, thanks to Tom McDevitt and Jeanne Theismann, dear friends who gave me the idea to write this book in the first place.

Foreword

The teenage years are a time filled with difficulty and confusion. For most, it is a period of discomfort and self-doubt, coupled with a deep yearning for love and acceptance. Teens would like the approval of their peers, to fit into a world that they do not yet understand. All too often, this desire to "fit in" leads to risky behaviors that can set a young life on a path toward destruction.

Young people need a support group of friends, role models, and adults, which they can turn to for answers, understanding, and leadership. Unfortunately, in a culture that often romanticizes and even encourages promiscuity and drug and alcohol abuse, support groups that help in making sound decisions are not often available.

Standing With Courage: Confronting Tough Decisions About Sex should make a difference in the lives of America's youth by offering them the support and leadership they need for a bright future. By taking the reader through the journey of her life, Mary-Louise Kurey engages young people and reassures them that they are not alone.

Her clear, warmhearted style conveys an important message for young people seeking answers in today's culture. She shares the trials she experienced and the turmoil she saw around her in her teen years. In doing so, she shows teens that the decisions they make today, if made wisely, will lead to rewards later. The lessons she has learned and the clarity of her position will help young people develop the courage to make the right decisions.

Mary-Louise Kurey aptly points out that saying "no" to sex, drugs, and alcohol is saying "yes" to life! This philosophy is what the Best Friends Program, an abstinence education curriculum that I developed in 1987, teaches youth.

The Best Friends program was developed with encouragement from my husband, Bill Bennett, former U.S. Secretary of Education and author of the *Book of Virtues*, as well as from my colleagues and friends. At the request of local school leaders, the program becomes part of a school curriculum. Beginning as a pilot program in the Washington, D.C., public schools, the Best Friends curriculum is currently taught to over five thousand adolescents in twenty-six cities in the United States and the U.S. Virgin Islands. Our recently begun program for the boys, Best Men, is being field-tested in Washington, D.C., and Milwaukee, Wisconsin. With the invaluable support of individuals such as Mary-Louise Kurey, Best Friends has played an important role in helping young girls, and now young boys, make healthy decisions.

As a national spokeswoman for the Best Friends Foundation, Mary-Louise has shown teens that being cool does not mean giving in to peer pressure. Her message of hope culminates with a simple yet life-changing philosophy that so many teens and even adults fail to grasp. It is a philosophy found in one of our Best Friends messages, "Tomorrow is the first day of the rest of your life." Past mistakes do not mean that one must continue in the same pattern. I believe each one of our youth has something positive to offer our society if he or she has the opportunity for sound guidance and direction.

In *Standing With Courage: Confronting Tough Decisions About Sex,* our young people will find a friend who understands the issues they face today, the courage to stand for what they believe, and a call to fulfill their unique mission. In our Best Friends program, our credo is "The Best Friend to have is that person who makes you a better person." After reading her inspiring and enlightening book, I believe Mary-Louise Kurey is truly a *Best Friend* to the youth of today.

— Elayne G. Bennett,
President and Founder
Best Friends Foundation

Introduction
Invitation to a Journey

I'm a virgin! This surprises a lot of people, especially when they find out that I'm twenty-seven years old. And when they discover that, as Miss Wisconsin, I spoke to over a hundred thousand teens and young adults about sexual abstinence until marriage, almost all are astounded, yet curious. What could have compelled me to do such a thing, and how is my message received?

I must admit that this vocation of mine is so unique that I'm surprised myself. I never imagined that someday I would be making my private life so public, and speaking frankly about things like sexually transmitted diseases, abortion, and contraception before thousands of people every month. But the Lord works in wonderful and amazing ways and has truly blessed me in my life.

I want to share with you my heart, my story, and most of all, my message. It's a message that needs to be heard, a choice that needs to be recognized. Each one of us deserves to know that when it comes to our sexuality, we're dealing with something beautiful, fragile, and precious. It is so precious that it's worth saving for that person who has made a lifetime commitment to love you unconditionally. Nothing is more special!

I've experienced the pressures of growing up in a sex-saturated society — a society that, on one hand, views sex as the essence of meaning and self-worth and, on the other hand, treats it as something ordinary and unimportant that we can throw around without consequences. I've also seen the depressing trends of broken homes and failed marriages that pervade our society today. It seems like everywhere we turn, we see married couples who appeared to be truly in love separating and divorcing. We see people who don't even believe in the institution and covenant of marriage any longer. Our modern culture lulls us into thinking that a good marriage is just luck, like a roll of the dice in a board game.

But these ideas are wolves in sheep's clothing. They're not just deceptive but dangerous. They can lead people into placing faith in "feel-good" relationships based only on physical attraction and "warm fuzzies," rather than on a strong foundation of love and true friendship. Some people use less care in choosing whom they give themselves to than what car or computer they'd like to buy. Many people view divorce as a viable possibility and an easy solution when they head into a marriage, rather than seeing marriage as a permanent and sacred commitment. Most of all, our society's lack of respect for sexuality and marriage causes many teens and young adults to question whether abstinence until marriage is worth the sacrifice, since happy marriages appear to be so few and far between. "What's the point of waiting, if my marriage is going to break up anyway?"

The actions that accompany these ideas come with consequences — painful consequences that stay with people for the rest of their lives. I witnessed in the lives of two close friends the devastating and irreversible consequences of premarital sex. The goals and dreams of these intelligent and talented young women quickly became a distant memory, and their lives today are filled with regrets. Their shattered dreams were the instrument that God used to compel me to speak out for chastity — so that others don't have to pay the same price and suffer the same devastation that my friends did. This work, so unexpected in my life, was a calling that I never wanted. In fact, I fled from it! But it has brought me great joy. It's amazing how the Lord took these tragedies in my friends' lives and salvaged from them many good things. It teaches us that we must have hope, no matter what happens in our lives. God is much more powerful than the adversity we face here on earth. Remember that He says, "I give them eternal life, and they shall never perish" (John 10:28).

One thing that I try to do is to live my life without regrets. Every single person I've spoken with who has had sex outside of marriage — regardless of that person's gender, age, financial situation, or ethnic background — has regrets. Such individuals wish that they hadn't done it. Of course, not all of them had regrets right away. But a week, a month, a year, five years, or even ten years down the road, they had serious regrets about their choice to participate in premarital sex.

With regard to my choices in my dating life, I have no regrets. In fact, I feel fulfilled! I'm not saying that abstinence is easy. But the most rewarding things in life never are! I know what it is to be tempted, to be pressured, and to be laughed at. But I also know the saving strength that God gives me each day to live out His truth. He believes that each of us, regardless of our faith, convictions, or past actions, is worthy of the best. He wants our lives to be free of the sadness that comes with out-of-wedlock pregnancy, sexually transmitted diseases, emotional scars, and low self-worth. He calls you and me by name and yearns to instill in our hearts the empowering knowledge that there is something better out there than the empty promises that society, with its cheap regard for sexuality, tries to push on us. God promises that what He holds in store for us is a crown worth winning — and it's won through our sacrifice. St. Paul points out that "no eye has seen, nor ear heard, nor the heart of man conceived, what God has prepared for those who love him" (1 Corinthians 2:9). Our Lord longs to give each of us the joy and self-respect that comes with the self-knowledge and understanding that "I'm worth waiting for."

Regardless of your background, age, or past choices, your sexuality is absolutely a *beautiful* and *precious* gift! It's so beautiful that it's meant for no one less than the person who makes a commitment to love you fully and unconditionally for a lifetime! There is no better choice that you can make than to embrace chastity, whatever walk of life you're from.

Perhaps you're thinking, "This is great for other people. But it's too late for me, because I've already made the wrong choice." Hear me now: You can put down this book, and keep doing what you're doing. And there are serious costs and serious consequences that you will have to face. Or, at this moment, you can open your heart to something better, by *making a new beginning* in your life. You can join the literally thousands of teens and young adults in our country each day who are making the commitment to a "secondary virginity."

You can't change the past. But you can decide what you're going to do today, and tomorrow, and the next day, and the day after that. Making a new beginning is tough — it's not going to be easy. But you will never regret taking this leap of faith — opening your life to empowerment, freedom, a happier dating life, and a better marriage in the future. When you start down this better path, you'll be tempted, but you'll never look back. May this book help you on your journey to healing and self-forgiveness, and may it give you the courage and strength to take control of your destiny.

Whether you've been living an unchaste lifestyle, are living out chastity in your life, or haven't yet faced this decision, I hope that this book will help you to discover your own personal mission and instill in you the understanding that you indeed are *precious*, and that your life has great purpose and extraordinary meaning!

Will you come on this journey with me? I ask you to read with an open mind and an open heart, as I share with you my story . . . How I made the commitment to wait . . . What motivated me to speak out for chastity . . . My experiences competing in the Miss America program . . . The excitement and fear of taking my message into unfriendly arenas nationwide . . . And the many moments of joy, frustration, hilarity, and sadness that filled each day as I brought the message of abstinence and character development to students in schools, churches, youth groups, universities, and conferences all over America. My life has been transformed! It's been an amazing journey. And it would be an honor to share this journey with you.

1

My Commitment

As a seventh grader, I was a pretty typical student. There were certain things that were important to me. One was to be liked — to be popular! I cared very much about what my peers thought of me, and their ideas dictated a lot of how I dressed and acted, what I said and whom I chose as friends.

I also had a few long-range goals. I loved to sing; I knew that this was something I wanted to do for the rest of my life. I loved to run, and I was fast. My seventh-grade school record of a 6:02 mile still stands! Someday I wanted to be an Olympic champion in the mile and two-mile. I wanted to go to college. With two older brothers already in college, I knew that education was not only important for my goals — it could be fun, too. And most of all, I just wanted to be happy.

And starting out in the seventh grade, I was pretty happy. My family was very loving and supportive. Although we had our arguments like every family does, my parents and my grandmother always made us know how much they loved us. My older brothers and sister were my best friends — not that we didn't give each other a hard time sometimes! But underneath it all, we knew how much we meant to one another. And the older we got, the fewer arguments we had, and the closer we became.

In seventh grade, I started to think that my mom and dad knew hardly anything at all. I thought that they "just couldn't relate" to what I was going through at school. I didn't feel that I could come to them with some of the problems and the issues I was dealing with. Unfortunately, it took me almost two years to realize that I was wrong!

To be honest, I headed into seventh grade as a pretty naïve girl whose life was mostly bike rides, sleepover parties, *Choose Your Own Adventure* books, the swim team, and — my favorite — performing in front of people. I couldn't stand it when my brothers called me by my nickname "Bunny" in public, and I was tired of being whaled on by my older sister!

I was totally unprepared for what was ahead. Had I known what was in store for me, I probably would have tried to turn back or join early the infamous IRTGU group my friends formed in high school. (This stood for "I Refuse to Grow Up!")

My First 'Test'

The first shock happened within a week or two of the beginning of the school year. My locker was next to that of a young man who was extremely handsome and very popular, whom I'll call "Brian." Brian always wore the latest fashion — his family had a lot of money. He was a lot of fun to be with. He was funny and outgoing, and within a couple of weeks, I considered him to be a friend.

But then I started to wonder about Brian. All of us liked to get to school early to meet up with friends. Brian was always there before me. He would spend about half an hour or forty-five minutes before school making "deals" with his friends. Many of them were in our homeroom. As I was hanging up my jacket and pulling out my books before classes, Brian would collect money from classmates and distribute small plastic bags with a tiny bit of white powder inside. I later learned that it was cocaine.

One morning, a couple of months into the year, he offered some to me. It was free the first time, he said, just to try it. After all, trying doesn't hurt anything, and we should all be open to new things.

My heart pounded as I considered his well-worded and harmless-sounding offer, and the half-smile on his tanned and friendly face. What he said sounded right — we should all be open to new things. I believed that. Trying new things, I knew, was usually a good thing. Most of all, Brian was my friend.

But then I remembered what I was thinking about doing. I knew what I had heard about drugs. I knew that I didn't have to try them to know that it was the wrong thing to do. I thought about my goals, my future, and my new friends. I also thought about all the money that people paid Brian for those drugs. It was a lot of money. Even if I wanted drugs, which I didn't, where would I get money like that? I thought about their emotionless faces, their bad language, their weird personalities. "No thanks, that's just not me," I said.

Suddenly, my quiet, fairly happy social life became very difficult. I had never been a member of the in-crowd, but I hung out with my own friends and it was no big deal. Now, I was the one that the in-crowd loved to hate, and they humiliated and embarrassed me in front of other people all the time, especially classmates and teachers. My clothes, my hair, my voice — they criticized everything about me. I was made fun of, ridiculed, and despised by some of the most popular students in my class. Of course, my "friendship" with Brian came to an abrupt end. He tormented me even more than the others, and it was his comments that hurt most of all.

I started to feel incredibly lonely. I dreaded going to school. I tried to arrive at the last minute, to avoid meeting people in the hallway who might make fun of me. When the five-minute bell rang before class, I'd walk into my homeroom, sit down at my desk, open a book, and hope that no one came over to talk to me — because if someone did, I knew it was just to make fun of me. I was very unhappy, and I started thinking and feeling badly about myself.

In our school musical *Coming of Age*, I had a short solo in a song called "If I had a Friend." It was about a girl who was very lonely and wished that she had a friend, and all of the fun things that she would do with her friend if she had one. I secretly wondered if I had been typecast in this role. I thought, "Is it that obvious to the teachers that I don't have any friends?"

True Friends

But even though I didn't realize it, I did have friends, including a wonderful new friend who was really smart, fun, and outgoing, named Jill. Her handwriting was really pretty, she got great grades, she had a beautiful voice, she was a great pianist, and she had a big role in the school musical. I wanted to be just like her.

But the peer pressure was starting to wear me down. I was tired of being picked on in front of my classmates all of the time. I was tired of feeling like an outcast just because my locker happened to be next to that of a drug seller and I refused to use drugs. I had endured just about enough. One day, I said to Jill, "You know what? Maybe I should just use drugs. Because if I do, I'll have friends, and I'll be accepted, and then I'll be happy."

Jill almost always wore a smile. But at that moment, her smile disappeared. She looked hard into my eyes, and she said to me, "In ten years, you won't even remember those kids' names. But while they're trying to put their lives back together from using drugs, you're going to be making something of your life."

Jill came from a tough family situation. Her parents were divorced, her older brother had been thrown out of the house, and her mother, with whom she was very close, lived hundreds of miles away. But she didn't let these things make her insensitive to other people or use them as excuses to do poorly in school. She knew what was important. And most of all, she knew what it was to be a good friend.

We all have "friends" like Brian who encourage us to make poor choices. As you go through life, you'll meet people who you think are friends and who pressure you to do things that are wrong. Whether it's using drugs, drinking underage, slacking off in school, cheating, acting disrespectfully to your parents and other adults, smoking, being violent, or having sex before marriage — all of these choices come with very serious consequences. These so-called friends know that these choices come with bad consequences. And they know that if you do what they say, you'll have to face those consequences some day.

But frankly, they don't care about that. They don't really care about your future, your goals and dreams, or your character — the kind of person that you become. Instead, they're thinking only about themselves. They're thinking, "I'm making a bad choice. But if I can get this person to make this bad choice with me, then my bad choice looks better. I look better!"

That's not a true friend. That's not the kind of person who wants what is best for you. That's not the kind of person who is going to stand by you when things get tough. A good friend is someone who helps you to make *good choices*. Real friends care about your future and your dreams. They want you to become the best that you can be.

Jill taught me a lot. She taught me that using drugs was stupid. She taught me to stick to my convictions and not to compromise my beliefs for popularity. She taught me to always think of things long-term, rather than getting caught up in the unimportant moment. By the way she lived, she taught me how to be strong and persevere, even when things are hard. But most of all, she showed me what it means to be a true friend.

She'll probably never know what a difference she made in my life.

Realization

The next shocking revelation in seventh grade was when I realized that my classmates weren't only doing drugs and drinking . . . they were having sex, too! At first, I thought it must be a joke, and I wouldn't believe it. Heck, I didn't even know very much about that stuff yet. They were probably just *saying* that they did it.

Maybe it was just talk. But by the end of seventh grade, I had a pretty firm belief from what I'd heard and what I'd seen that a number of my classmates were involved in sex. Now, don't get me wrong — not everyone was having sex. Only the most popular, super in-crowd was. They were the only ones "daring enough" to go all the way.

I was confused. Was there something wrong with me? I didn't want to have sex. And I didn't want to smoke or drink or use drugs either.

By the second half of seventh grade, I had more friends, and I was running really well in track. I had started my singing lessons, too, and they were a lot of fun. All these things seemed to tell me that I was okay. But then why did I feel so lonely and empty inside?

That feeling of isolation and emptiness was one of the best gifts of my life. I didn't know it, but God was using it to invite me to a deeper relationship with Him. In my loneliness, I would gaze into the eyes of the picture of Jesus in my room, and He would look back at me lovingly. I turned to the One who knew what it was like to feel alone and friendless — for He was despised and rejected by His own people. He even called out to His own Father on the Cross, "My God, my God, why hast thou forsaken me?" (Matthew 27:46).

I discovered in Jesus a kindred spirit, a friend. Suddenly, going to church on Sunday wasn't a chore — I even kind of liked it, and found myself looking forward to it on the weekends. I started to pray more often, remembering how I would see my brother John sit in his room and pray. I thought about how Mom and Dad would gather us around the Advent wreath for prayer each night during those four weeks before Christmas, to prepare our hearts to welcome Jesus into the world. And I slowly returned to my wonderful childhood habit — I started to "talk" with God, telling Him my problems, my fears, and even the things I didn't understand that were happening to me. Sometimes I felt Him listening! In my mind, I knew that He was always there.

The Mustard Seed

Then God chose to reveal Himself to me through one of my favorite languages — music. At the end of the year, I was sitting with the seventh-grade chorus at the final concert, listening to the eighth-grade chorus perform. "They're really good," I thought. Then our chorus director, Mrs. Albers, turned around from conducting the choir to speak to the audience. The last song of the concert was a very special piece, she said. A teacher had written this song in memory of a student of his who had died of a drug overdose. Mrs. Albers said that every year, the eighth-grade graduating class at our junior high school performed this song, and she told the seventh graders to listen to it very carefully, because this song was saying something especially to us.

Here are the words of this song, "Walk a Little Slower, My Friend," by Don Besig and Nancy Price, which had — and continues to have — such a tremendous impact on my life:

Walk a little slower, my friend,
And take a little time along the way.
We don't need to borrow any moments from tomorrow —
There's so much here for us today.

Walk a little slower, my friend,
And try to hear what people have to say.
Search to find a meaning, 'cause there's more to life than
*   dreaming.*
We have to find a way to face it, every day.

So when you see the sun come up each morning,
Be thankful for the brand new day that's dawning.
A time to grow . . .
A time to show that you alone can make a difference.

Think it over, my friend.
Don't pass it by or let it slip away.
Grab your chance and take it —
Life is only what you make it.
Start here and now to live it — every day.

The time has come to make a new beginning!
If you believe, you have the chance of winning.
Keep aiming high . . .
Reach for the sky,
And do your best to make things happen.

Think it over, my friend.
Don't pass it by or let it slip away.
Grab your chance and take it —
Life is only what you make it.
Start here and now to live it, every day.
Just live your life, every day!

As I listened to this song, I felt like I was coming out of the fog of confusion in my life, as if Someone was granting to me a vision of my future, my purpose, and my meaning on this earth. This song was speaking directly to me! I needed to "walk a little slower" — I was always rushing through life, eager to be called an adult and to grow up, trying to get things over with. I needed to "search to find a meaning," to seek a purpose and a meaning in life beyond who the most popular person was this week or what I was going to wear. I took to heart the words "Grab your chance and take it — Life is only what you make it." My life was filled with joy and opportunities — it really was a gift! I had dreams and goals — and I needed to go after them. I needed to "live my life every day" — not just exist or react to things around me, but *live!*

In my heart, something was saying to me, *"The time has come to make a new beginning."* A few days after that concert, I was

lying in bed, where the Holy Spirit often visited me with inspiring thoughts, even though I didn't know it. I was thinking
about my life. I was thinking about my future — my goals and
dreams, and things that I wanted to accomplish. I was thinking
about my family — my loving parents, my two older brothers,
my older sister, my grandmother, and Pop, who was looking
down on me from heaven. And I was thinking about Jesus and
Mary, my best friends, who had given me so much and covered
me with their mantle of protection against all of the temptations
and confusing things that I had faced that year.

At that moment, quietly, in my mind and heart, I made a
commitment. I promised to myself and to Jesus that I wasn't
going to drink underage, smoke, or use drugs. But most of all, I
promised that I was going to wait — that I wasn't going to have
sex outside of marriage. I promised to keep myself chaste for the
fulfillment of my vocation, whatever it might be. I made the
commitment to a life of chastity.

I don't think I really understood just how important that
moment was — or what a tremendous impact it would have on
the rest of my life.

Jesus had planted a mustard seed in my heart.

2

Chastity: Why? What Is It?
And What's the Big Deal?

Another parable he put before them, saying, "The kingdom
of heaven is like a grain of mustard seed which a man took
and sowed in his field; it is the smallest of all seeds, but when
it has grown it is the greatest of shrubs and becomes a tree, so
that the birds of the air come and make nests in its branches."

— MATTHEW 13:31-32

How was my commitment to chastity, which I made when I
was twelve years old, like the "mustard seed" of my life? Why
was this promise — which seemed sort of small and embarrassing at the time — so unexpectedly important in the long run?
How does it bring me so much happiness?

As I look back, I know that it was only with Jesus' help that I
made this bold and empowering choice — one that would bear
great fruit for the rest of my life! I know this because I was not a
girl with a "naturally" strong character, who would often stand up
for what was right. I was easily influenced by others and often
swayed by my peers to do things that were spineless instead of
doing what was good. But God took my weakness and transformed it into resolution! He gave me the courage and insight
that I needed to take this firm stance — to "stand strong" and to
be a *rebel for truth*.

When I look back at the girl in seventh grade who made
this commitment, I remember that there were three things in
my life that compelled me to choose the best. What's amazing is
that, fifteen years later, these three things are still the most
important aspects of my life. As you read them and think about

your own life, perhaps you'll find that deep down inside, these "Three F's" are close to your heart as well!

The First of the 'Three F's' — My Family

The first reason I embraced a lifestyle of chastity was for my family — my family of the *present*, and my family in the *future*.

One of my favorite early childhood memories is of my grandfather —Pop — brushing my hair. I would come in from being a tomboy, playing outside, and my hair was almost always in a tangled mess. Since it went well below my waist back then, this was a pretty big problem. My sister would call it "a rat's nest"!

My mother, who worked very hard taking care of all of us and had very little time, would take a hairbrush and quickly try to make me look presentable. Of course, this would pull my hair, and I would cry out in pain! But then Pop would take the brush from her and, sitting me on his lap, he would brush my hair very slowly and carefully. We would call it "one strand at a time." I remember that many times it would take more than an hour for him to untangle my disheveled hair!

In this and hundreds of other little ways, my family let me know that I was precious to them. My parents sacrificed so much of their time and money to give me the very best that they could. My brothers and sister treasured me — they protected me on the playground and on the school bus, and they surrounded me with fun and excitement. My grandmother showered me with love, support, her constant prayers, and words of inspiration each day. Nana always believed in me.

I knew their expectation — that I would not have sex until I was married. It was unspoken . . . they never sat us down and told us this (although I wish that they had!). They said this each day in their actions. They would carefully monitor the programs I watched, what I was doing with friends, how much time I spent on the phone, and what books and magazines I read. They got to know my friends, and later on, they got to know the guys

I dated. My mother always insisted on knowing specifically where I was going, with whom, and what time I was coming home. Although this drove me crazy, I knew deep down that my parents did these things because they loved me.

I couldn't imagine how horrible it would be if I had sex and they found out about it. Even one time would hurt them deeply, and it would be completely unacceptable. My mother spent countless hours discussing issues with me to develop my mind and character. Something like that would be a huge breach of trust, because she believed that I was always open and honest with her. What about my brothers? They would probably beat up the guy! Could anything be worse than having to tell Nana that I was pregnant outside of marriage? What about my sister? She would never look at me the same way. What would Pop think, who was up in heaven praying for me? And my dad . . . Well, I didn't even want to think about that!

One Choice Impacts Many

You see, when a couple has sex before marriage, they're not only affecting themselves. They're hurting their parents, brothers and sisters, grandparents, uncles and aunts, cousins, friends, and anyone else who looks up to them or cares about them.

That young woman is someone's daughter. Someone taught her how to read, held her hand as she crossed the street, dreamed of what she would achieve someday, and made countless sacrifices to give her the very best. She's a precious treasure! She is a role model to her brothers and sisters, cousins, classmates, work colleagues. Her friends look up to her and are influenced by what she does.

That young man is someone's son. Someone bandaged his skinned knee, cared for him when he was sick, showed him how to throw a baseball, and gave him the very best that they could. He is a tremendous gift! He's someone's brother, someone's cousin, and someone's mentor. He's someone his friends look to for guidance, and they follow what he does.

Now, even if you don't think that these things are true about you, they are! Whether you're an only child or in a family of ten, whether you're twelve years old or twenty, and no matter how terrible or wonderful your family life is, you are *precious* and *loved*. Whether you realize it or not, you are loved by many people, and — more powerfully and specially than you can possibly imagine — you're loved by God! Your life touches many people in an important way each day!

Wouldn't it be silly — or downright dumb — to jeopardize all of these precious relationships? Wouldn't it be sad to risk losing the positive impact that you make on the lives of the people you care about, by making a bad choice?

Your Future Family Is Waiting!

Several months ago, I started dating a wonderful young man. One night, we were having a lot of fun, talking for hours about really deep subjects, really getting to know each other. I asked him if he was a virgin. He paused, looking down. Then he said to me, "You deserve an honest answer, and I could never lie to you. I'm not a virgin. I've made mistakes in my past — I've done things that I'm not proud of."

I sat silently, thinking about what he said. I was disappointed and surprised. Then I said to him, "But why didn't you wait? Why didn't you wait for me or whomever you're going to marry?"

He said, "I didn't know you were going to come along."

When this terrific guy had sex outside of marriage, he didn't just hurt himself and his partner. He didn't just hurt both of their *present families* — parents, grandparents, brothers, sisters. He hurt their *future families*, too.

He took something that wasn't his — the precious gift of that young woman's virginity. That belonged to her future husband or to the fulfillment of her vocation. And she took something that wasn't hers — the precious gift of his virginity. That was meant for the person that he will spend the rest of his life with or for the fulfillment of his vocation.

Someday, I'm going to give my husband a great gift! I'm going to say to him, "I love you," not just with my *words*, but with my *life!* Because I waited for him! And I hope that he will have waited for me, too, so that he can give me the same precious token of his love. I may not know who my husband will be, but I'm already loving him, by the way that I'm living my life.

Someday, we'll have to answer for our actions to our children. Someday, your son will question you, "Dad, did you wait?" Your daughter will ask, "Mom, did you stay strong?" What are you going to tell them?

I know that as a seventh grader, I didn't understand the importance of these factors as fully as I do now. But just as God reveals to little ones the mysteries of the Kingdom, God revealed to me back then that chastity is not only the best choice that I can make for my *present* family — it's the very best gift I can give to my *future* family as well.

The Second of the 'Three F's' — My Future

The second reason I chose chastity was for my future — my goals and dreams, and the things that I wanted to do with my life. I was aware of the fact that sex outside of marriage comes with very serious consequences. Out-of-wedlock pregnancy, sexually transmitted diseases, painful emotional scars — all of these things can easily prevent young people from achieving their dreams and fulfilling their potential.

God had planted some dreams in my heart. I wanted to run in the Olympics, perform onstage, graduate from college. Although I didn't really know it at the time, God had a hand in these dreams. These goals of mine were things that could give Jesus a lot of joy — if I did them to glorify God and bring happiness to others.

Some of these dreams have come to fruition in my life, like

performing onstage and graduating from college. Other dreams, such as running in the Olympics, haven't come true, and probably never will. And new dreams have replaced old ones — like becoming Miss Wisconsin, a wonderful experience that changed my life forever.

Chastity has empowered me to achieve many of my early dreams, for two reasons. First, I have avoided negative consequences like the ones I mentioned above. And second, I have received many wonderful gifts and blessings from this commitment, like self-respect, strength, integrity, and courage. These qualities have become a springboard to accomplish new, even greater, dreams!

I know that if I hadn't made this commitment to chastity, I would not have become Miss Wisconsin. Of course, this isn't because the contestants had to fill out a "virginity questionnaire"! It's because this commitment is the essence of who I am and what I do. Without chastity as the ideal that I embrace each day, I would be a very different person. I wouldn't have the self-respect, perseverance, and broader view of life that has helped me to achieve my dreams. I would have had no motivation to compete in the Miss America program, other than to get scholarship money. I would have had no mission, no message to share with others, because although I didn't know it, this was the mission that God had in store for me. All I had to do was make the right choices and persevere.

Your Mission

> No one after lighting a lamp puts it in a cellar or under a bushel,
> but on a stand, that those who enter may see the light.
>
> — LUKE 11:33

God has given you a mission. God has given you dreams. Perhaps you already know what these are. Perhaps you're searching for them. Or perhaps you're just starting to think about it. Wherever you are on this journey, one thing is certain — you were born to make a difference in this world! No one is born to live a life without meaning or a life of emptiness. Remember, Jesus said, "I came that they may have life, and have it abundantly" (John 10:10). My friend, you were born to accomplish things that only *you* can do! You were put in this world to contribute something that only you can give!

Now you might be thinking, "Come on! Let's be realistic! There are so many people in this world who are good at the same things I'm good at." This could be true. Perhaps you're good at math, or you play the flute very well, or you're a great baseball player, or you have a terrific sense of humor. A lot of people are good at those things. But they don't come from the same perspective that you come from. They haven't had the same experiences that you've had. They don't have the same insights and understanding that you have.

I don't care where you come from, what your family is like, what mistakes you've made or how popular you are. *You were born to make a difference in the world!* Every time you say no to sex before marriage . . . every time you say no to drugs or violence or underage drinking or cutting school, you are saying *"yes"* to the rest of your life!

You're saying *"yes"* to your future. You're saying *"yes"* to your dreams. You're saying *"yes"* to the different opportunities that await you. You're saying *"yes"* to living life to the fullest. You're saying *"yes"* to making a difference in the world. You're saying *"yes"* to living your life with no regrets!

My grandfather used to say that every child is born into the world with a *message*, a *light* tucked in his hand — a light that only that child can bring! But if that child is lost, either through abortion or through not fulfilling his or her potential, then that light is lost to the world forever.

Whether you know it or not, your personal mission is vital to this world. And God has given you special gifts and talents to fulfill your mission — and to achieve your dreams. Maybe you're a very strong, courageous person, or perhaps you're a talented pianist. You might be a terrific basketball player, or very compassionate toward others, or maybe you're an excellent writer. There are all sorts of interesting and unique gifts that God gives each of us.

God didn't give you these gifts to hide under a bushel basket, concealed from the world. He gave you these gifts to use to the fullest! He wants you to place your talents on a lampstand so that your light will shine for the whole world to see!

Your Dreams Are Precious!

Our goals and dreams — the things we want to do with our lives — are a way to use these gifts to the fullest. But when we make poor choices that come with serious negative consequences, we risk losing these fragile dreams forever. Premarital sex is one of those choices that can hurt — and even destroy — dreams.

Two friends of mine had been given special gifts and talents, just like you. They were put on this earth for a reason, to bring their special light to the world. They had goals and dreams — things they wanted to achieve in their lives, and things that they held close to their hearts. But because of their choice to have sex outside marriage, their dreams were shattered. Today, those goals are just a distant memory. Their lives are filled with regrets. (I will share their stories with you in later chapters.)

Speaking to tens of thousands of teens and young adults all over the country, I've heard hundreds of stories of heartbreak resulting from the consequences of premarital sex.

I can't express it strongly enough — *watch over your dreams!* They are a glimpse of your mission, your special light to bring to the world. And they truly are *precious*.

The Greatest 'F' of All — My Faith

The third and most important reason that I made this commitment to chastity was for my faith. I knew that living out my convictions would be difficult, and that I wouldn't have the strength and courage to stick to this decision without God's help. Most importantly, I knew that God was calling me to live out chastity in my life.

At this moment, God is calling *you* to live out a lifestyle of chastity as well! It doesn't matter what your background is, your religion, what your family is like, or what choices you've made in your past. God is lovingly inviting you to embrace this commitment in your life. He's asking you to choose the best — to choose chastity. Because by living out chastity in our lives, we're able to truly love others the way that Jesus loves us!

This is the main goal of life: To love, and to be loved — with a *real* love! Not the self-centered, wimpy, temporary "love" we see on *Dawson's Creek* or *Friends*, but a real, powerful, giving, fulfilling, lifelong, deeply spiritual love!

Called to Be a Rebel

Shun immorality. Every other sin which a man commits is outside the body; but the immoral man sins against his own body. Do you not know that your body is a temple of the Holy Spirit within you, which you have from God? You are not your own; you were bought with a price. So glorify God in your body.

— 1 CORINTHIANS 6:18-20

I must admit that my faith is not nearly as strong as it should be. But it's still the center and stronghold of my life. My faith is the source that everything in my life flows from — my choices, my personality, and my happiness.

In seventh grade, my faith was the faith of a child. Today, it's still in the growing stage; it's like a plant beginning to sprout from the soil, to enjoy the air, and to reach toward the sunlight. At my age, that's not so great. No, I'm not a "great" soul. And so I turn to Jesus and bury myself in His love and mercy. He gives me the strength and courage that I need each day to live out His loving challenges.

He strengthens me to show you and others that even the least of His souls can be made strong! If I can make God's teachings the stronghold of my life, so can you! You can "stand strong" and be a *rebel for truth* in our society today!

Remember when people were criticizing Jesus' apostles for not washing their hands before they ate? It's always a good idea to wash your hands before eating, but the Lord used this opportunity to emphasize that it's not what is external that makes a person bad or dirty or corrupt; rather, it's what comes from inside that corrupts a person. Jesus instructs us to "clean the inside of the cup, so that the outside will also be clean." In other words, living out purity on the inside flows into our external actions. He invites us to follow Him, for His yoke is easy, and His burden is light.

Does this mean that chastity is always easy? No! It's tough. But so is anything that is really worth going after. If you're striving be an Olympic champion, class valedictorian, a great musician, or the President of the United States, you know that you need to put in a lot of hard work. The same is true in striving for courage, integrity, strength, self-respect, and a great future.

As I was on a plane, traveling to a speaking event, I happened to get into a conversation with a young woman sitting next to me, who asked me about my work. She was around thirty years old. She told me that she thought that my work encouraging students to live out chastity was great. She admitted that she'd had sex before marriage. Even though she ended up marrying her partner, and he was the only man whom she had given herself to, she said that now she truly regrets having had sex with him before their wedding night.

"I'm not going to make any excuses," she said. "I knew that what I was doing was wrong. But we wanted the instant gratification that comes with sex — the physical pleasure and the emotional closeness. I guess we thought we knew better. It's too bad."

I Knew That What I Was Doing Was Wrong

Those are strong words today. No one likes to say that anything is actually "wrong." "A bad idea," perhaps, or "not a smart choice." But "wrong"?

Today, society tries to tell us that there is no such thing as right or wrong, except in each individual's mind. In other words, there is no such thing as "truth" — there are only *relative* opinions or perspectives.

No matter how relativistic our society tries to be, we know that there is such a thing as right and wrong. It's right to form your conscience, stick to your convictions, practice self-control, and be a person of integrity, self-respect, character, and courage. It's right to make some sacrifices in the present moment for a fantastic future. It's right to be a *rebel for truth.*

What Exactly Is Chastity?

In order to examine the role of chastity in our lives, it's important to ask, "What exactly is chastity, anyway?"

Throughout my life, I've learned that chastity is not just abstaining from sex until marriage — although abstinence is a great and essential part of chastity. But abstinence implies "not doing something" — a passive role or a negative approach. Chastity, on the other hand, is a *call to action!* It is an active, deliberate lifestyle choice to embrace purity of mind, heart, and body, and to use this choice as a way to shape your character and discover your mission!

Chastity is a lifestyle that one actively pursues each day with enthusiasm. It's respecting the sacred — yes, sacred! — bodily frame that God has given you. It's respecting the beautiful gift of your sexuality.

Chastity doesn't ask, "How much can I do before marriage and still technically be called a virgin?" Rather, it asks, "How much can I save for my future spouse, and for Jesus?"

You're a Chalice

Imagine that you are at a party with a priest who is drinking Coke out of a beautiful chalice all night. Then as he's leaving, he says, "Well, I guess I'd better wash this to use for Mass tomorrow morning." That would be pretty offensive. Why? Because he took something sacred — a special chalice that holds the Body and Blood of Jesus — and he used it as if it was something ordinary, like a Coke can.

Now, if we consider that chalice — an inanimate object — to be sacred, *how much more sacred are you?* That chalice wasn't made in the image and likeness of God! That chalice wasn't baptized in the name of the Father, and of the Son, and of the Holy Spirit. That chalice doesn't have a soul that will live forever. Remember, the Lord says that "even the hairs of your head are all numbered" (Matthew 10:30). He knows every intimate detail about you and cares about every small aspect of your life, because He loves you passionately!

My friend, you are truly sacred! You are so sacred that God chose to make you in His own image, unlike any other creature that ever has existed or ever will exist in the entire history of the world! God lovingly calls you His son or His daughter. You're more precious to Him than to your parents, grandparents, boyfriend or girlfriend, siblings, or friends. St. Paul says "that your body is a temple of the Holy Spirit," and gives you and me a challenge, to "glorify God in your body" (1 Corinthians 6:19, 20).

That sounds like a pretty high calling. But what does that really mean? I think that it means treating our bodies with the respect that God accords to them. After all, God is the only One who knows everything, and He considers our bodies to be very special, even sacred. He wants us to treat our bodies with the respect that they deserve, by making the commitment to chastity.

We show a commitment to chastity in the way that we walk and talk, the TV shows and movies that we choose to watch, the music that we listen to, the way that we dress, and the way that we treat other people in our relationships. All of these are opportunities to actively pursue and nourish chastity in our lives!

I'll be honest with you. It isn't easy. Each passing day, I learn more and more of what it means to be chaste. Chastity needs to be lived out, so it's always "a work in progress." But the rewards for growing in chastity are abundant! They even surpass your imagination!

A few years ago, I had no idea that I would be given the opportunity to speak with tens of thousands of teens across the country, to reach millions of people with this message, to write a book, to compete in the Miss America Pageant, and to represent the beautiful state of Wisconsin for a year. These are gifts that have been given to me by God, to reward my commitment to Him, and to further His plan through me.

If you choose to embrace chastity, you also will be rewarded a hundredfold for your sacrifices and struggles! The investment is small, but the return is amazingly great! Once you start down this path, you will appreciate yourself and others more, and you will never look back.

A Reality Check

Now, maybe you're thinking, "This sounds great for *her*, but things are different for me." Maybe your friends are making fun of you for being a virgin. Maybe you don't know anyone who is married, and you think that you don't want to be married either. Maybe you feel so tempted that you don't think you'll ever be able to be chaste. Maybe you're longing for that special feeling of emotional closeness or belonging or excitement that your sexually experienced friends tell you about. Maybe you've already had sex. Maybe you're in a sexually active relationship right now.

Let's be real. Think about all the pressures out there to have sex. It doesn't have to be explicit — it can be very subtle. Let's think about the daily conversations of our classmates or colleagues. Let's think about the music we hear on the radio . . . the headlines of magazines we see on store racks . . . the movies, TV shows, and music videos that we see or hear discussed many times each week. After all, we don't live in a vacuum. What we see, hear, and read each day affects us.

How can God, who loves us so much, ask us to do something so difficult? Why would He want to deny us the pleasure of giving love to someone else in this beautiful way? Why does He want us to go against what society tells us is "natural"?

Casting Out Into Deeper Waters

A few days ago when I was at Mass, the Gospel described how Jesus called Simon Peter and his friends James and John to become disciples. Although I'd heard this story many times, it struck me in a new way.

> Getting into one of the boats, which was Simon's, he asked him to put out a little from the land. And he sat down and taught the people from the boat. And when he had ceased speaking, he said to Simon, *"Put out into the deep and let down your nets for a catch."* And Simon answered, "Master, we toiled all night and took nothing! But at your word I will let down the nets." And when they had done this, they enclosed a great shoal of fish; and as their nets were breaking, they beckoned to their partners in the other boat to come and help them. And they came and filled both the boats, so that they began to sink. But when Simon Peter saw it, he fell down at Jesus' knees, saying, "Depart from me, for I am a sinful man, O Lord." For he was astonished, and all that were with him, at the catch of fish which they had taken; and so also were James and John, sons of Zebedee, who were partners with Simon. And Jesus said to Simon, "Do not be afraid; henceforth you

will be catching men." And when they had brought their boats
to land, they left everything and followed him.

— LUKE 5:3-11 (EMPHASIS ADDED)

It hit me, as I listened to this familiar passage, how this story
parallels Jesus' loving call to chastity in our own lives!

We are constantly exposed to the allure of a sex-saturated
culture, to the idea that our sexuality is merely a vehicle for fun
and status. Perhaps we've struggled with chastity. Perhaps you're
like many of my friends, who thought that sex was the answer to
helping a troubled relationship, and then saw that relationship
end painfully. Perhaps, like some of my friends, you have gone
from one partner to another in search of Mr. or Miss Right.

And then maybe, like some of my friends, you got a wake-
up call. They hopped off the treadmill of failed relationships to
take a closer look at their lives. When they were alone, away
from other people who were "doing it" and the provocative TV
shows, movies, and magazines, they realized that they really hurt
inside. They didn't understand why. The glamour, fun, and happy
relationships that society guaranteed would come with premarital
sex were just empty promises. Even with great intentions of
finding the right person, and trying hard to meet people and
make relationships work, they were like the fishermen in Luke's
Gospel: "We toiled all night and took nothing!"

But then, they took the leap of faith! They risked going
out "into the deep." Like Peter, who couldn't understand Jesus'
request but did what He asked anyway, many of my friends
said "yes" to God's loving invitation to chastity without really
understanding why. They renew this "yes" each day! It isn't
easy, especially for those who had been sexually active. Some
of these friends didn't think about the role that God has in
their lives. They didn't know that He was inviting them to lay
down all the pain and burdens that come with premarital sex
to make a new beginning. They just knew that premarital sex

had left them with a lot of heartache and problems, and they hoped that chastity would bring them more happiness than their past choices.

For their leap of faith, their casting out "into the deep," their "yes," they have been rewarded abundantly! God has brought them so many great blessings! He has started to use each of them in such a powerful and wonderful way, so much so that "their nets are almost breaking" with happiness. They are surprised by the fresh, positive direction their lives are taking, the happy and uncomplicated dating life they've discovered, and the sense of peacefulness and self-worth that they've gained.

They have found themselves again. Rather than identifying themselves by what their boyfriend or girlfriend thinks or how many people they've slept with, they have discovered their own identity and see the great qualities they can bring to the world. They are realizing their own personal "light" and fulfilling their mission.

They have also found out what is truly important in male-female relationships: friendship, trust, common interests, respect, joyful self-sacrifice, great conversations. They have reclaimed their sense of chastity and the beauty of their sexuality. They have experienced an increase in self-respect, courage, and strength. They've discovered that true riches are won through sacrifice.

It's Your Turn to Go Deeper!

Sometimes Jesus asks us to do things that we don't understand. Sometimes He asks us to do things that are hard or even scary. Jesus says to you and me, "Put out into the deep." Do we want to leave the safety of the shoreline? Do we want to place our faith in an idea that is so countercultural, like chastity? Do we want to make a choice, a promise, a commitment that is going to require such great sacrifice?

Imagine what would have happened if Peter had said to Jesus, "No, we won't go out deeper — we already did that and didn't catch anything." Or if he had said, "No, my friends think that's silly, it's a waste of time," or, "Sorry, but we're too busy to do that." He and his friends would have missed out big time! They could have gotten to know and follow God's Son, but they chose to pass it up! Their lives would have continued in their humdrum way and they never would have known what they missed. Instead, Peter chose to take the leap of faith and cast out deeper, even though he had doubts about it and didn't really understand why.

It's hard to take that leap of faith, especially if you have doubts. But when you do, God rewards you in incredible ways! And the blessings aren't just for now — *they last a lifetime!*

If you choose to accept Jesus' loving invitation to chastity, you will be able to hold your head high and truly be proud when you look at yourself in the mirror. Rather than being plagued by regrets, you will be bringing your own personal "light" to the world and achieving your mission. You'll have discovered your vocation, and it will bring you lots of happiness. And you'll be able to say, "Even when things were tough, I stood strong. I was a leader. I didn't compromise my beliefs — I did what was right. I stood with courage."

What Is My Vocation? How Do I Know?

Now there are varieties of gifts, but the same Spirit.

—1 Corinthians 12:4

A person's vocation is the individual way in which that person is called to serve God and others. It's also the lifestyle that will give that person the greatest happiness. Each of us has a special and unique vocation, based on the different gifts and talents God has given each of us. Your vocation is the way God calls you to live your life, and when you discover it, you'll find your greatest level of happiness.

This is what I mean when I say "the fulfillment of your vocation." It's carrying out the special calling that God has given you.

There are four types of vocations. Each one is beautiful in its own way and each can be difficult at times. With each vocation, there are different types of crosses to bear and different types of joys. Each of us is called to one of these four vocations: married, religious, clerical, or single life.

Chastity encompasses all four of these vocations.

Chastity in the married life means saving the gift of your virginity for your future spouse and having sexual relations exclusively with that person for the rest of your life. "Therefore a man leaves his father and his mother and cleaves to his wife, and they become one flesh" (Genesis 2:24). This is what the *sacrament* of marriage is. It's not an artificial institution that people made up! It's a sacrament that God created for our happiness and to help us fulfill our potential. God unites *three* — the husband, wife, and Himself — into *one* sacred bond forever. Sex consummates (completes) that joining. So when a married couple has sex, they give themselves to each other, not just physically, but spiritually and emotionally as well. You've made a lifetime commitment to that person; you give yourself completely to your spouse, and she or he gives herself or himself completely to you. This is why we were given the beautiful gift of our sexuality, and it is the best way you can experience it, because it makes you one with your wife or husband for a lifetime.

Chastity in the religious life means becoming a religious sister or brother and consecrating the beautiful gift of your sexuality to God, practicing celibacy as a sacrifice to glorify Him. This imitates the lifestyle that Jesus practiced when He lived on earth, and it's a special calling. Some people don't understand this; they think that because Catholic nuns, priests, and monks are celibate, the Church is saying that sex is bad. It's just the opposite. If sex were bad, it wouldn't be a sacrifice to give it up. But because sex is so wonderful, the act of giving it up to serve God in a special way is a tremendous gift to God; it can fill a person with great holiness and help such a person to stay focused on serving God and others.

Chastity in the clerical life means becoming a priest or deacon and living out chastity by taking on the Church as one's spouse. This is similar to chastity in the religious life, in that it involves celibacy for priests. But deacons who are married, of course, share the gift of their sexuality with their spouse. The primary difference between the vocations to the clerical life and the religious life is that in the clerical life, the priest is espoused to the Church — the Church is his "bride." In the religious life, a sister or brother is espoused to Christ.

Chastity in the single life is, I believe, the most difficult of the four vocations. This is a vocation that we all have for at least a little while in our lives. This is where I'm at in my life right now, and where you're probably at also. This means living in the world as a single person, and practicing chastity. This can be a stage that ends when a person gets married — or it can be a person's ultimate vocation. Not everyone has a calling to be married, or to be a religious brother or sister, or to be a priest or deacon. The vocation to the single life is just as important as these vocations.

Although the single life sounds difficult, if it is your true vocation, it is the vocation that will bring you the greatest happiness. This lifestyle gives a person a special opportunity to serve God in the world in a very visible and important way. Because single people aren't raising families or living in religious communities, they have more time and flexibility to "take Jesus to the streets" in our mainstream culture today.

I turned twenty-seven in October of 2001, and to tell you the truth, I'm not yet sure what my vocation is! But that's okay. God chooses to reveal these things to us at His appointed time. Right now, I'm living out chastity in the single life. But perhaps someday I'll get married or become a sister, if this is what Jesus calls me to. Sometimes God reveals a person's vocation when he or she is only six or seven years old; and sometimes He waits a long time before he lets a person know what his or her vocation is. Perhaps you already know your vocation. But if you don't, that's not a bad thing. God will reveal this to you through prayer and the events of your life.

You might want to say this simple prayer: "Jesus, grant me the wisdom to discern my vocation and the courage to carry it out." (A priest once shared that with me, and I think it's really great! I try to say it every night before I go to sleep.)

Sometimes people's vocations change as life goes on. For example, a close friend of our family was a young adult during and following the Great Depression. Her family was impoverished, and she ended up caring for her mother and remaining single. Although she was disappointed, she made peace with the fact that she would never marry. Then, when she was in her upper forties, she met a wonderful man whose family situation had been similar. He also had never been married and had resigned himself to being single for the rest of his life. They fell deeply in love and got married. And their marriage was filled with great happiness and joy until he passed away more than twenty-five years later.

Whatever your vocation is, one thing is definitely clear: God is calling you to make the very best choice that there is — the choice that comes with no regrets and enables you to live life to the fullest. God is calling you to a life of chastity.

You're not reading this book by chance. God is speaking to you at this moment. Perhaps He's saying to you, "Come home. And I will set you free." Let this choice be the mustard seed of your life. Take a risk — put out into deep waters. Sometimes it will be hard. Sometimes it will even be scary. But you will be amazed at the abundance of rewards you'll gain for your sacrifice.

If you feel in your heart that you want to make this commitment to chastity, or if you've already made this commitment and want to renew it to make it stronger, I invite you to take a moment to find that quiet place in your heart for God. Allow your brain to stop whirling and forget about everything around you. Just focus on Jesus, your very best friend. Enjoy that peace. And then, if you wish, offer this prayer:

> *Jesus, open my heart, and help me to realize how precious I am to You. At this moment, give me the courage to take a great step in my life, to "Put out into deep waters." From this day forward, I make the commitment to a lifestyle of chastity, whatever my vocation may be. I ask You to give me the courage, strength, and joy each day to carry out the beautiful plan that You have for my life, and to discover my own personal light to bring to the world. Amen.*

3

New Friends and a Wake-up Call

Go therefore and make disciples of all nations, baptizing them in the name of the Father and of the Son and of the Holy Spirit, teaching them to observe all that I have commanded you; and lo, I am with you always, to the close of the age.

— Matthew 28:19-20

When you stop learning, you stop living." This is a common pearl of wisdom in our American culture, and I think it's definitely true! High school was a special time in my life when I learned a lot, not only from my classes at school, but also from the friendships that I made through my involvement in the arts. My new friends were interesting, wonderful people. Some of them challenged what I believed. I was faced with a choice that all of us must face — should I be "open-minded," or should I stand with courage? I needed a "wake-up call" to answer this important question.

'Closet' Virgin

People are often surprised by how open I am about my private life. One thing my friends find pretty funny is that I have no problem walking into a room full of people and letting them know that I'm twenty-seven years old and a virgin!

But I wasn't always so open about my commitment to chastity or so encouraging of others to join me in making this choice. As I mentioned before, for a long time I felt embarrassed about this commitment — and maybe even a little ashamed of it.

When I entered high school, I didn't have many friends, and I would have died of embarrassment if my classmates had known about my commitment to chastity. This shows how weak I really was. I needed an excuse to hide my beliefs. So I began to tell myself that what other people did was none of my business. "Even if they're having sex before marriage, their choice is just as valid as mine," I would try to convince myself.

When I began high school, I thought that I was prepared for what was ahead. I thought that I was ready to conquer my new school in academics, sports, and the arts. I was leaving my large suburban junior high school behind, a school filled with sex and drugs, to enter a Catholic high school in the city of Milwaukee, the largest Catholic high school in the state. I couldn't wait to make the jump.

Pius XI High School gave me a great education in everything from academics to spirituality, from its awesome fine arts program to its competitive sports teams. I love to go back and visit because of all of the special memories of my times there, the friends I made, and the teachers who deeply touched my life.

But like every high school, it also had its problems, not only with sex and drugs —which weren't any worse than what I'd experienced — but with cliques among the students. I thought that my adjustment to middle school was hard . . . but it was nothing compared to high school.

Most of the students were from small Catholic grade schools. Rather than being eager to make new friends, they clung to their own elementary school groups, which competed for status on the high school totem pole of popularity. No one was really interested in being friends with a girl who had no status and didn't know anybody.

I was gangly, awkward, and not very attractive. After eighth-grade graduation, I had decided to get a "grown-up" hairstyle. As long as I could remember, I'd had very long hair that went halfway down my back. I couldn't wait to cut it off! Unfortunately, I didn't realize how curly my hair was. My new, short hairstyle stuck out all over the place. Combined with my braces, skinniness, and latest growth spurt, I was almost a pathetic sight. As I became more of an outcast in school, my personality became more introverted and insecure.

At the end of my first semester at Pius, I still spent most of my lunch hours eating alone. In a school of over seventeen hundred students, there were only three people whom I could even attempt to call friends. On the other hand, there was a long list of students who loved to pick on me and humiliate me in front of my classmates, especially in my biology and religion classes. I was miserable and depressed; I felt badly about myself.

Surprise!

My mother noticed my unhappiness and encouraged me to focus on the upcoming auditions for the school musical *My Fair Lady*. I fell in love with the movie, memorized it, worked on the accents, prepared my audition song, and prayed every night to get Eliza, the leading role! I really took to heart Jesus' promise that "every one who asks receives, and he who seeks finds, and to him who knocks it will be opened" (Luke 11:10). Little did I know how much Jesus would take pity on my loneliness and hunger for a new challenge!

The Holy Spirit had helped me in a great way during the auditions. On the day that the cast list was going to be posted, my heart pounded as I ran up to the sixth floor, with my coat and backpack flying behind me. As I neared the top, I saw a crowd of angry upperclassmen talking loudly. They became strangely quiet as I approached the list. Resentment hung thickly in the air. Then I saw it.

ELIZA   MARY-LOUISE KUREY

I was ecstatic! But the rest of the school was infuriated! People wrote letters to the school newspaper objecting that a freshman got the lead. Some demanded that I give up the role. One upperclassman even threatened to push me down the stairs! After-school meetings were called. Parents were outraged. Students quit the show to protest. Teachers discussed it in their classes. Students, parents, faculty, and administration were swept up in the controversy surrounding a quiet, unpopular freshman.

The role was a blessing that God had bestowed on his lowly servant (me!). Although many people made my social life hard, I didn't feel that it could be any worse than it already was. I made it clear that I wouldn't give up the role. I started to gain friends, mostly among the wonderful upperclassmen who chose to stay in the show with me. We became so close that it was as if they adopted me like a little sister. In turn, I looked up to them like my older brothers and sisters and aspired to be like them. God broke down my wall of loneliness and filled my life with friendship, music, and joy!

A New Mary-Louise

Each rehearsal and each time I practiced at home, I offered up my efforts to the Lord. I gave God the little that I could in thanks for the great blessings He had showered on me. In return, He gave me a confidence that I had always longed for but never thought was possible. I felt some kind of transformation happening inside of me. I even looked different, as my hair had grown out into a more attractive style and I walked through the hallways with happiness in my heart. I was becoming the person that I wanted to be.

On opening night, the performance was sold out, with an audience numbering well over a thousand. The gymnasium floor, bleachers, and balcony were jam-packed with people. Those of us buzzing around nervously backstage could hear the din of laughter and muffled conversations as the audience waited with excitement and anticipation for the curtains to go up.

As I stood in the wings, focusing on the performance ahead, I marveled at the way that God had changed my life and at the many gifts He had given me.

Peeking through an opening in the curtain, one of the seniors said to me, "We've never had a crowd like this before. The whole school is here. I wouldn't want to be in your shoes for anything."

I smiled. Although I couldn't sleep the night before (my lines and songs went buzzing around and around in my head), I felt surprisingly peaceful. I was remembering when I was about four years old, standing on a kitchen chair making meatballs with my grandfather while we listened to opera records. I knew that Pop was up in heaven, watching over me. He had inspired my love of music long ago. Tonight, I was performing for Jesus — and for him.

Backstage, everyone else was tense, including the directors! They had paid a political price to cast me in this role. I could tell that they were wondering, "Will this little freshman come through?" The other students watched me as they heard the impatient shuffling of the audience. Most of the people really hadn't come to see the show. They had come to see the freshman that caused all the commotion.

In spite of these pressures, the Holy Spirit kept any doubts from crossing my mind that day. I knew that He was going to be with me every note, every line, every step of the way. I didn't feel alone — I felt joyful.

The first performance was unforgettably wonderful, truly a magical experience for me. And from that point on, although I was never "popular" in school, I never lacked friends.

New Friends, Different Values

Cain said to Abel his brother, "Let us go out to the field." And when they were in the field, Cain rose up against his brother Abel, and killed him. Then the LORD said to Cain, "Where is Abel your brother?" He said, "I do not know; *am I my brother's keeper?*" And the LORD said, "What have you done? The voice of your brother's blood is crying to me from the ground."

— GENESIS 4:8-10 (EMPHASIS ADDED)

As a variety of people became interested in getting to know me better, I became much more open and accepting of different types of people. I had many friends from a variety of groups, who had different values and diverse backgrounds.

There were my "artsy" friends, who were into music, theater, dance, or visual arts. There were my "super-smart" friends, who were in the accelerated, college-prep classes. There were my "athletic" friends from cross-country and swimming. There were also my "burn-out" friends who were in the creative writing club, had purple or green hair with words shaved into it, body piercings, and should have owned stock in various tobacco companies for the countless cigarettes they smoked.

It sounds like a strange combination of people, but my high school was so large — and had so many great extracurricular activities — that many of these groups actually overlapped. I loved my different groups of friends, and I enjoyed throwing many parties, bringing all of them together to form a very diverse, unusual combination of people!

Their different values intrigued me. Although my junior high school had been large, there were only two grade levels, and all of us had grown up in the same area. My Catholic high school, on the other hand, was right in the city of Milwaukee and had seventeen hundred students from all over the suburban and metropolitan area — students who came from a wide variety of backgrounds and values.

I enjoyed the diversity of my school — and the diversity among my friends. Many of my friends were very much in favor of legalized abortion, extremist/anti-Christian art, drug legalization, and anything that a person felt was right in his or her own conscience (as long as it went against traditional values). As I adopted their beliefs, I felt that I was becoming very open-minded and enlightened. I had moved beyond the "narrow-minded" values of my parents. I had broadened my horizons.

Although I never saw it, I suspected that some of my friends were drinking, using drugs, and having sex. In fact, although my high school was a terrific place to get an education and socialize, one of the sayings that went around our school was, "Nobody graduates still a virgin." But I felt that this was okay. After all, I had come to believe — as my friends did — that whatever a person does, if such a person believes that he or she is doing the right thing for himself or herself, then it's okay.

I was so proud of myself for having become so tolerant and accepting. I was wonderful! I was enlightened! My friends' choices were different from my own, but their choices, I felt, were just as valid as mine. After all, wouldn't it be close-minded of me to force my beliefs on them? Besides, who was I to tell them what to do?

Am I My Brother's Keeper?

Recently, a young man and I were discussing programs that distribute condoms in schools. I told him that I preferred sex education programs that promote abstinence rather than the so-called "safe" sex education programs that ignore the emotional and psychological consequences of sex outside marriage. He rudely cried out, "Now you want to get into people's bedrooms! You should just mind your own business. If you don't like what other people do, then stay at home, but don't try to force your opinions on the rest of us."

This type of irresponsible thinking was exactly what I believed when I was in high school! My friends' choices were not an issue to me. I brainwashed myself into thinking that their choices — which sometimes included drinking, using drugs, and having sex — were equally acceptable in comparison to mine.

"Even though drugs, drinking, and premarital sex aren't right for me, who am I to say that it isn't right for *them*? After all," I thought, "it would be very close-minded of me to not accept their differences. Who am I to force my values on them? And how is what they do any of my business? Am I my brother's keeper?"

It was then that I received a wake-up call from God.

Sarah's Story

It was the summer after our freshman year of high school. I enjoyed getting together with my friends, most of whom were in the same summer theater camp. We would go to the pool, the movies, the zoo, the beach. We had a wonderful time, sharing life and growing up together.

For several weeks, we met at a burger place after theater camp each afternoon. Six or eight of us were usually there, including a friend I'm going to call "Sarah." She was smart, outgoing, and fun to be with. She joked around a lot and had many friends. She liked foreign languages and she loved kids. She wanted to be a teacher. She also had been dating the same guy for what we considered to be a long time — several months.

But after the camp ended, Sarah stopped coming to meet us. She never joined us for pizza, a picnic, or the zoo. She didn't even return our phone calls. When school started up again, we saw Sarah, and we all asked her where she had been. "I had a baby," she said, kind of laughing. We thought she was joking, and tried to laugh along, even though it wasn't very funny.

But when she pulled out the baby pictures, we realized that she was telling us the unbelievable truth.

None of us could understand how we hadn't noticed that she was pregnant. "I always wore baggy clothes," she said. Looking back, I realized that she had never come with us to the pool or the beach, where she would have to wear a swimsuit. But her secret was incredible.

"My parents didn't even notice. The first time my mom found out was when I woke her up in the middle of the night and said to her, 'I'm having a baby. Take me to the hospital.' You should've seen the look on her face," Sarah laughed. This time, none of us were laughing.

We couldn't believe that her poor little baby didn't have any prenatal care. "I read books on that stuff, and watched what I ate and everything. But you're right," she conceded, "that was pretty dumb." Fortunately, her little girl was healthy, although very small. Because of Sarah's young age, her baby "Molly" was placed with a foster family.

We soon realized that Sarah's flippant, almost joking way of talking about things related to her daughter was really her way of trying to conceal the anxiety she had experienced during the nine months of her secret pregnancy — and the real emotional and psychological pain that she was enduring as a teen mother.

One day, as a group of us sat in the cafeteria, she started crying. "I just don't understand," she said. "This wasn't supposed to happen. They told us that we were safe." Sarah said that she and her boyfriend used condoms every time they had sex.

Some of the guys in the group who were sexually active looked at each other, shocked. "This could have happened to any of us," one of them whispered.

Difficult Choices

Although we all wanted to forget about it, we soon realized that this wasn't something in Sarah's life that was going to go away. She thought continuously about what she was going to do about Molly. Sarah had grown to love her little girl during the nine months that she had secretly carried Molly inside of her. Sarah had gone through a painful, difficult labor to bring a beautiful little girl into the world. The thought of being separated from her daughter for the rest of her life was unbearable.

But then, what were her choices? Should she take Molly from the foster family, bring her home, and raise her as a sixteen-year-old mother? Sarah wondered about the goals and dreams she had imagined since she had been a little girl herself. She wanted to go to college. She wanted to be fluent in many languages. She wanted to travel to Europe, to experience different cultures and peoples. She wanted to be a teacher.

Sarah loved her little girl. She missed her. But what about her own dreams?

She thought about placing Molly with a family through adoption. This was what her parents and the social worker wanted her to do. After all, Sarah had a great life ahead of her, filled with so much promise, so many possibilities. And it was for the baby's own good, they contended. How could a sixteen-year-old be a good parent? Molly would bring an adoptive couple so much joy! Sarah could even be involved in choosing the parents.

One day, as Sarah was tearfully wading through her choices during lunch, one of the guys in our group said, "That baby is yours. You have a right to be with her. I think you should go and pick up that baby from the foster home and raise her yourself."

All the guys agreed. We girls looked at each other — and said nothing.

I know that I should have said something, but I didn't know what to say. If she had been my baby, I probably would have placed her with a family in adoption. I know many married couples that are longing to adopt a baby and can't find one. These loving people with stable lives and careers would be much better parents than I would have been as a sixteen-year-old single mother.

But I also knew that Sarah's only happy days were the days when she went to visit her little girl. Without Molly, Sarah seemed to find no joy in life.

Reality Sets In

A few days later, Sarah brought her daughter home from the foster family to keep her permanently. Her parents were furious — they threw them out of the house. Sarah and Molly had nowhere to go.

They stayed at a friend's house for a week or so. Then they

moved in with Sarah's boyfriend and his mother. His mother was a truly wonderful woman. She was a great blessing to them during this difficult time. His mother cared for their baby while they went to school. Because of this sacrifice, Sarah and her boyfriend were able to graduate from high school. Sarah was one of the lucky ones. Studies show that only three out of ten girls who get pregnant before they are eighteen earn their high school diploma by the time they are thirty.

Of course, we never saw her — or her boyfriend — when we went to the dances, to the pep rallies, or even when we went out for coffee. When they weren't at school or studying, they were working hard in order to afford the many things that Molly needed, like diapers and formula and doctor's visits. When they weren't doing that, they were taking care of their little girl. They didn't have time to have fun with us anymore. We all got a glimpse of what it was like to be a teenager and a parent. And we didn't envy them.

I remember when all of us graduated; Sarah's parents didn't come, but her boyfriend's parents did, and they brought Molly. She was now almost two years old, and she was adorable!

Sarah told us that she and her boyfriend were going to move out on their own. "His mom has been great, but she said it's time for us to take responsibility and raise her by ourselves. We'll be fine," she said. "With both of us working, it shouldn't be too bad. After all, we're both pretty smart, and we really love each other."

Our group agreed. If anyone can do it, I thought, it's those two.

Unfortunately, things didn't go as well as we had expected or hoped. Since they couldn't afford day care, Sarah and her boyfriend had to get jobs working opposite shifts, so that one of them would always be home to care for their daughter. They also tried to take a college class at a local campus, slowly working toward their degrees. They rarely saw each other or were able to spend quality time together. They struggled to make ends meet. Sadly, they couldn't pull through, and their relationship ended.

Sarah's reality today is so very different from what any of us had imagined her future would be like. She was given so many gifts — her caring, outgoing personality; her intelligence; her sense of humor; her love of foreign languages; her adventurousness; her love for kids. She was going to travel the world, graduate from college, and become a great teacher. She was going to touch the lives of thousands of students and make a difference to so many people.

But unfortunately, Sarah hasn't realized her dreams. Today, she works in a job that doesn't use her talents and abilities, a job where it's difficult for her to make ends meet. She hasn't been able to achieve her own personal mission. She hasn't been able to bring her own personal light to the world. She hasn't fulfilled her promise.

Because of a choice that she made when she was fifteen years old, Sarah's life will never be the same. Sarah said to me, "I love my little girl. *But I wonder what my life would be like now if I'd waited.*"

She wishes that she had waited. I wish that she had waited, too. She is a very special young woman. Her life was so filled with promise. Her heart is so warm and kind and giving. She deserved the best.

And you deserve the best, too.

Regrets

Today, Sarah's life is filled with regrets. Perhaps what makes it even harder is that she knows that she could have had the life that she wanted — she could have achieved her dreams. Her dreams were in the palm of her hand. But her dreams were shattered by a choice that she made when she was fifteen.

Sarah isn't the only one who has regrets. I have regrets as well . . . I'm left wondering, *"If I had said something, would Sarah's life be different today?"*

By not speaking with my friends about chastity, I believed

that I was being "open-minded." I thought that I was enlightened. I felt that I was so accepting of other people's values, although they were different from my own. I wasn't "forcing my opinions on anyone." I believed that if a person does what he or she believes is right in his or her own conscience, then that makes it right. I thought that this relativistic thinking was a "broader view" of life.

But now I see these ideas for what they are. They aren't noble, educated, or truthful. They are selfish and cowardly. I used these ideas to justify my silence. I didn't want to tell others about my commitment to chastity or my true feelings about drug and alcohol use, because I was afraid. I didn't want to be rejected. I didn't want to be made fun of. I didn't want to take the trouble of sticking my neck out. I didn't want people to say that I was forcing my opinion down their throats, like that young man told me years later. And so I took the easy way out. I silently stood by as my friends made destructive choices, while I made sure that I took good care of myself.

That wasn't "open-minded." That was wrong.

A scholar once said that our society has become so open-minded that our brains are falling out. He's pretty funny. But he's also right. Although my brains hadn't physically fallen out, I had forgotten my sense of right and wrong. I had forgotten that there are absolutes. The concept of right and wrong isn't based on people's opinions, and it's not based on being "open-minded." It's based on truth.

Sarah's experience was the first wake-up call God used to break my silence. I say "the first," because, even though Sarah and Molly's lives haunt me to this day, it wasn't enough to make me change. I heard God faintly in the distance, asking me to speak to my peers about chastity, to stand with courage. But I chose not to listen, because I didn't believe that I was strong enough.

Sarah taught me a lesson. *I am my brother's keeper.* And, my friend, so are you.

4

The Empty Promise of Popularity

Blessed are those who are persecuted for righteousness' sake, for theirs is the kingdom of heaven.

Blessed are you when men revile you and persecute you and utter all kinds of evil against you falsely on my account. Rejoice and be glad, for your reward is great in heaven.

— Matthew 5:10-12

It's hard to take a stand. And it's even harder when you're surrounded by people who will try to make your life miserable if you do.

In middle school and high school, it was very important to me to be liked by my peers. As I said before, their opinions strongly influenced the way I acted, how I dressed, whom I hung out with, and what I said. I wanted to be popular. Being "persecuted for the sake of righteousness" was not my idea of a good time.

But I soon realized that when I tried to make everyone like me by changing who I was, I was losing myself. I was compromising my beliefs. I was acting out the role of a person who wasn't me. And I felt even worse when I thought that people liked this made-up person better than they would like "the real me," if they knew the person that I truly was. There was always that underlying feeling: *"They wouldn't like me if they knew who I truly am."* That's a really heavy burden to carry alone.

It's an easy trap to fall into. It might start with something small . . . then before you know it, it develops into something larger, until you've created an image that isn't who you really are. From that point on, that's how people expect you to be. You feel trapped.

The only way to escape is to take "a leap of faith," to shed the persona that you've taken on and to reveal your true character to the world. Whether you're Miss Popularity or Mr. Body Piercings, it's frightening to drop the mask of your made-up image and be the person that you are — a child of God who is growing into the person you are created to be. It means that you're making yourself vulnerable to others, by revealing to them your true self and standing up for your convictions.

During the summer before my junior year of high school, I gradually came to the realization that I couldn't pretend any longer — I had to be the person that I really am. I decided to take a leap of faith and just be myself. I found that I was a lot happier, and I discovered something wonderful and important. I realized that there were a lot of people who liked me and accepted me for *who I was*, and that these people were my true friends. Even though other people sometimes made fun of me or didn't like me because I wouldn't do things that would make me "popular," I was very happy. Because I found that *my worth didn't come from what other people thought of me, but from striving to be the person that God made me to be.*

This is a great lesson! This is the revelation that I hope you and every teen and young adult discover! It doesn't matter what other people think of you or how popular you are. It doesn't matter if you're the MVP on the football team or you're the prettiest girl in the class. It doesn't matter if you're the class clown, the smartest kid in the class, or the best pianist your school has ever seen. It doesn't matter if you're class president, or hang out with really popular people, or hold the school record in the long jump. Those things are great, but they're all so minor in comparison with what's really important! Those things have *nothing* to do with how important or valuable you are as a person.

You are important and precious because you are a child of

God. His love doesn't depend on what you do — it's about who you are! No matter what you've done in the past, at this moment, sitting right where you are, God is lovingly calling you by name. He is calling you His "son" or His "daughter." That is what makes you awesome!

As we discussed earlier, God has a special mission and purpose for you — something that will bring you a lot of joy in your life! Remember, Jesus said you were not created to die, but to "have life, and have it abundantly" (John 10:10). Each day, whether you know it or not, God is with you, wanting to help you achieve your own personal mission. All you have to do is ask!

And so when people make fun of you for who you are, Jesus has a surprising response. He says, "Blessed are you." He says, "Rejoice and be glad," because you're staying true to your convictions. You're fighting on the front lines of the culture war that is happening in our society today. You're a *rebel for truth.*

You don't have to go out of your way to be like everyone else. And you don't have to go out of your way to be different, because you already are. You don't have to try to please everybody or to impress others. All you have to do is please God, who is already madly in love with you and wants your ultimate happiness!

One of my favorite quotes, which I read on the wall of a Christian teen center, is: *"The only applause that I seek is the applause of nail-scarred hands."*

What a cool saying! It puts everything in perspective. It's something that we can remember each day to remind us of what's really important.

I wish that one of my best friends had discovered these truths in high school. She is a very special and gifted young woman. But she jeopardized everything to seek popularity and approval from her peers. In doing so, she almost lost herself.

Susan's Story

I met "Susan" in history class shortly after the beginning of my freshman year. She was kind, intelligent, talented, caring, beautiful, and lots of fun to be with. She also was an excellent gymnast and competed on the best gymnastics team in the metropolitan Milwaukee area, with potential to make the Olympics. Susan also had high grades in all of the accelerated classes. We became fast friends and had fun opening our hearts to each other, sharing our dreams, goals, and lots of laughter.

Susan decided to audition for the cheerleading team at the end of that year. I knew that she would make the team and that she would be among the best, because of her talent and dedication. But I also knew what the social life of the cheerleaders involved and the type of crowd that they hung out with. On a positive note, they were one of the most popular groups in the school. But they garnered their status by making poor choices — most of them were heavily involved in drugs, drinking, and sex. I was worried about my friend, who was gentle, innocent, and kind.

Susan was thrilled to make the team, and she quickly rose to the top — literally! She often "topped off" the pyramids in their routines! But the time commitment was very hard on her, in addition to everything else she was doing. The cheerleaders practiced for five hours each day during the summer, and attended weeklong training camps. They also had competitions on the weekends. During the school year, they practiced like many sports teams, a few hours each day after school, with competitions and games at nights and on weekends. Susan realized that she no longer had time for her gymnastics team. She also started struggling to keep up in her classes. But she sacrificed these things, which were a crucial part of her long-term goals, to continue participating on the prestigious cheerleading team.

Students — especially young men — started to notice Susan.

Her beautiful smile, graceful movements, and lovely form attracted a lot of attention when the team performed at rallies and football games. When people got to know her gentle spirit, they were even more interested in becoming her friend. This quiet, little-known girl was quickly becoming one of the most popular students in our large school.

Of course, with all of her new friends and so many guys interested in her, Susan had less time to spend with me. Even though I missed her, I was happy for her. She had become a leader in our school. People looked up to her. And so did I.

But Susan was changing. Her laughter didn't come as easily any more. She didn't have the carefree, fun-loving spirit that I remembered. Instead of the soft smile that she usually wore, she now looked worried.

When we talked, we no longer shared our dreams and goals. These topics were replaced by mundane, short-term concerns: There was a "friend" on the cheerleading team who was annoyed that Susan was featured in one of the routines instead of her. A guy was spreading rumors about Susan because she wouldn't go out with him. She couldn't decide which party to go to next weekend or what outfit she was going to wear after the game on Saturday. Susan's life had suddenly become a lot more complicated — and more focused on the momentary than the lasting.

The cheerleaders hung out a lot with the football players. In our high school, they'd go out after the games, mostly to parties where there would be a lot of drinking and a lot of sex. Susan never liked to talk about what happened at these parties. She almost always went. But I really wonder whether she had very much fun.

Even her eating habits seemed to be changing. In the cafeteria, Susan would take out her sandwich and break off small pieces to eat very slowly. At the end of our lunch period, she'd throw more than half of it away.

She was starting to look at colleges. "I really want to become a pediatrician," she confided. "But I'd have to take two science classes next year to go pre-med, and with cheerleading, I just don't have the time."

At the end of the year, Susan was selected to be co-captain of the cheerleading team. She was also chosen to represent our high school in the solo division at the state competition. She was totally overjoyed. But the other girls, her "friends" on the team, weren't as happy for her. They would try to make things difficult for her at practices. Sometimes they would say unkind things behind her back. One time a teammate came to me to tell me something that Susan had supposedly said about me. Of course, I knew that it was untrue; she was simply jealous of Susan's accomplishments and popularity. (It was the only time that this girl ever lowered herself to speak to me! After all, I wasn't with the in-crowd.)

Susan returned for her senior year with the championship title. She won the state competition, and the team had taken many national awards over the summer under her leadership. She and the other co-captain had made up the cheers, planned the routines, rehearsed the team, and even selected the hairstyles and uniforms that the team wore. They were unbeatable.

Susan's popularity continued to soar. Each morning before school, she was surrounded by a large group of students in the hallway. Everyone wanted to be considered her friend. She was the one that every girl in the school wanted to be, and every guy in the school wanted to date. That fall, Susan was elected homecoming queen. But still, she seemed to be unhappier than ever.

"Who should I go to homecoming with?" she asked me. "I don't really like this guy, but everyone expects me to go with him."

"Go with whomever you want," I said. "Who cares what they think?"

She didn't respond, but I knew the answer — *she* cared. And she cared too much. She sometimes was even a little embarrassed to talk with me in front of her friends from cheerleading.

"You're my only real friend," she said to me one day.

"Oh, that's not true!" I protested. "You have a ton of friends here! Everyone in this school wants to be your friend!"

"But you're the only one who really knows me," she said. "You love me for who I am. When I'm with them, sometimes I don't even know who I am anymore."

It hurt to see her so unhappy.

As the year wore on, Susan and I saw less and less of each other. But we knew that we would always be there for each other — we were "soul sisters." Our friendship was a precious relationship that made us each stronger and more empowered. But eventually, I noticed that Susan was looking pale and very thin. It concerned me, and I mentioned it to my mother. "Susan has an eating disorder," my mother told me. "This has been going on for a while."

I couldn't believe it. My friend was the most popular girl in the school. She was talented, smart, pretty, and a wonderful person. And yet, she felt terrible about her body image, and worse about herself. This news made me want to bury myself in sadness, that my best friend was enduring such suffering, and I hadn't even known.

Toward the end of senior year, Susan was elected prom queen. It was the first time in many years that the same young woman had been chosen both homecoming queen and prom queen at our school. She had become almost a legend.

I went to the prom that year with my boyfriend, a young man that I'd started dating during the summer after our sophomore year. We were having a wonderful time together, with our own circle of friends.

Later in the evening, I caught a glimpse of Susan across the room in an unguarded moment. She was the queen, the star of the show. She was the center of attention. She was beautiful. But she looked very pale and worried. Her date — another guy she didn't really like — was joking loudly with his friends. She was looking around at everyone and no one.

And that's how she was a lot during those last two years of high school — always looking around to see what other people thought.

At that moment, I understood. I remembered the song, "On the Inside Looking Out," that a girl sang in our seventh-grade musical, *Coming of Age.* While all of the other students longed to be part of the in-crowd, this character, who was popular at school, sang about how unhappy she was to be trapped in her group:

> *On the inside looking out,*
> *They're having all the fun.*
> *While we crawl in our formations*
> *They can fly and they can run.*

I remembered when Susan's spirit *did* "fly" and "run." I remembered when we would sit together for hours, sharing our deepest secrets and our greatest dreams. I remembered her laughing and living and loving life. I remembered when we did what we wanted to, without worrying about whether or not it would make us popular. Our souls were like tender flowers that were just beginning to open to life, enjoying the freshness of the air and the warmth of the sun's rays.

I looked at her now. She looked like the girl that I once knew, but no longer with that spark, that shining inner light. Where were her quick smile and her fearless but gentle soul? Now, every word, every action, was carefully planned to consider what her classmates thought. Even her dates were based on other people's opinions.

Anxiety, drinking, an eating disorder, and true unhappiness.

What happened to the innocent and carefree days when we were unknown and unpopular?

Picking Up the Pieces

To an observer, Susan's high school experience looked like every young woman's dream. But in truth, it was a nightmare. It took her years to overcome the effects that high school had on her self-image, her spirituality, and her long-term goals.

Today, Susan has returned to her "true self." After struggling with various problems, she has become the young woman that she was created to be. She picked up the pieces of her heart, which was betrayed and broken, and made a new beginning. She looks back at high school as a very dark period in her life, when she made many choices that she now regrets. The "friends" that followed her around back then, advising her on the "popular" things to do and planning her social life, are nowhere to be found.

But our friendship still flourishes.

My friendship with Susan was never based on how pretty or how popular she was. It wasn't determined by what she did or how she acted or who her friends were. I cared about her for *who she was*, and who she would become as a young woman. She was no less "valuable" a friend or person when she was struggling in her life and facing a lot of problems. Our friendship is stronger now, because both of us have grown.

Susan is a great blessing in my life. And I'm so glad that after all these years, she has finally come home.

She teaches all of us something very important: to be true to ourselves. We should never compromise who we are to win popularity, because that kind of superficial friendship and esteem isn't worth winning.

Stand with courage. You'll gain happiness and self-worth from sticking to your convictions. You'll grow in your faith. And you'll find out who your true friends are.

Are You a Susan?

All of us have a tendency to be like Susan. We want so much to be liked and accepted among our peers that it can be tempting to sacrifice everything for the fun and prestige that comes with "having an image."

Whether you aspire to be the class clown, the most talented artist, the best jock, or the toughest Goth, you might be creating a mask to get other people to like or respect you.

But the good news is that you don't have to do that. You're not a square peg that has to fit into a round hole, although life can sometimes feel that way. Every single person has experienced those feelings at least one point in their lives.

A friend of mine was telling me about her five-year high school class reunion. "Everyone was talking about how unpopular they felt, how they didn't have any friends," she said. "Even the most popular people said that they felt lonely and insecure in high school."

It's normal to experience insecurity and loneliness, especially in junior high and high school. We all want to be liked and to please others. It's good to want to make other people happy. But when it's done at the expense of who you are, it's not just bad — it's wrong. God created each of us to be unique. When we try to be the same or pretend to be something we aren't, we're rejecting God's creation. We're not being true to ourselves.

A Search for Something Deeper

God calls us to something deeper than the superficial and temporary fame of popularity. He loves us with a *true, lasting love* — and calls us to share this love in our love for others.

No matter how important or unimportant you are in the world's eyes, whether you're reading this from your cell in a juvenile detention center or you're an extremely successful business executive, we all have one thing in common: *Each of us wants to be loved in a lifelong, meaningful, fulfilling way!* And each of us wants to *give* love in that way as well.

But we're human beings. We have flaws. We can be selfish and insensitive. Can we really love one another selflessly, faithfully, generously, and unconditionally for a lifetime?

Absolutely! Because God promises to help us.

> Jesus looked at them and said to them, "With men this is impossible, but with God all things are possible."
>
> — MATTHEW 19:26

Look at the couples you know who have been married for a long time and are truly, passionately in love with each other. In almost every case, their love is built on their relationship with God.

God's love is the highest model anybody can look for in love. He loves you fully and unconditionally. His love isn't dependent on what you do or how you look. God's love is deeper than the love of the most giving parent, grandparent, mentor, or teacher. God's love is more exciting than the most passionate relationship you can imagine. God's love is more accepting and forgiving than the love of the greatest brother or sister or friend.

That's because God's love is *perfect!*

This means that at this moment, where you're sitting right now, *no matter what you've done in your past*, God loves you to the *fullest!* He loves you passionately, so much that He died for you on the Cross! God's love is as enormous as the ocean, and it's all for you! He loves you so much that He can't love you any more intensely than He already loves you — the *ocean of His love* is already *overflowing!*

That's why when we surrender to God's love, we are the happiest, and we rise above our own limitations. When we allow God to be the central focus of our lives, we find our greatest level of fulfillment. And when we love God and accept His love, then we really find out what it is to love other people.

When you compare that to the type of popularity that is won through pretending to be someone you're not and doing things that are stupid, the answer is clear. God's love for you leaves everything else in the dust! That's why "God is love," because He created love and He is the Master of love. My friend, God loves you *so much!*

> *God, help me to know how much You love me, right here, at this moment, regardless of whatever I've done in my past. Give me the strength to resist the temptation to compromise for popularity. Help me to stand with courage, to stick to my convictions, and to fulfill the mission that You have given me. Lord, help me to truly love others as You love me. And help me to be able to wake up each morning and say with all my heart:*

> *"The only applause that I seek is the applause of nail-scarred hands."*

5

A Voice for the Voiceless

"For I was hungry and you gave me no food, I was thirsty and you gave me no drink, I was a stranger and you did not welcome me, naked and you did not clothe me, sick and in prison and you did not visit me." Then they also will answer, "Lord, when did we see thee hungry or thirsty or a stranger or naked or sick or in prison, and did not minister to thee?" Then he will answer them, *"Truly, I say to you, as you did it not to one of the least of these, you did it not to me."*

— MATTHEW 25:42-45 (EMPHASIS ADDED)

Although it started out pretty rocky, high school ended up being a fantastic time in my life. It was a time when I learned so much, not only academically but also spiritually. And I learned a lot about life.

When I walked across the stage to accept my diploma at the end of my senior year, I felt proud of what I had accomplished. Of course, there was room for improvement. But my classes had been difficult, and I had persevered. There had been a lot of peer pressure, yet I had stayed true to my convictions (although silently). I felt ready for my next step, moving away from home and attending college.

My college search turned out very differently from what I had hoped. I had always dreamed of attending an elite Ivy League school, and I worked extremely hard in high school to accomplish this goal. But when the time came for me to choose a college, my parents didn't have the resources to send me to any of the schools that I had originally wished to attend, yet we didn't qualify for financial aid.

Of course, I was very disappointed. I had worked so hard, and I had the grades to accomplish this goal. I had even prayed that I would attend a prestigious university. Deep down inside, I tried to trust in God. In my mind, I knew that God was still in charge, watching over everything and guiding me along the right path. We don't always understand why things happen, but things happen for a reason.

The University of Wisconsin-Eau Claire had an excellent music school, a gorgeous campus, and a fantastic private voice teacher whom I really admired. In addition, the scholarships that I received combined with the low tuition for state residents took most of the financial burden off my parents. God has a way of showing us that although His plan is sometimes different from ours, in the end, it is always far better!

Although none of my high school friends were going to UWEC, I was confident that I would be able to make new friends and enjoy the freedom of being away from home responsibly. I was looking forward to becoming the young woman that I wanted to be in a place where there was no label for the person that I was. I was eager to enter a new stage of my life.

My First Taste of College Life

My first college friends lived on my floor in the dorm. I didn't have very much in common with most of these freshman girls, but during the first week, when we had orientation, eight or ten of us would sit together in a room for hours and just chat. We were all eager to make new friends and enter into the full-ness of college life.

Soon our differences became apparent. Many of the girls were excited to go out to the house parties, where there was a lot of drinking, and meet guys — maybe even "hook up." A few of us weren't interested in doing that. We found a lot of fun things to do though, like walking over to the coffee shop, get-ting an ice cream, playing air hockey and darts with some of the guys in the dorm, organizing some late-night volleyball, or roller blading on the path along the river. Sometimes we would stay in and get a pizza, rent a movie, and talk. And usually, I would spend at least part of one weekend night studying or practicing in the music building.

Sometimes we'd see the other girls stumble in late at night, drunk and laughing. Other times they were drunk and crying. And sometimes they didn't come back at all. They loved to tell the rest of us about their adventures, and gossip about their other partying friends. I was amazed at how many of the girls lost their virginity during those first few weeks of college. Most of them didn't really intend to. They would go to house parties to have fun, get drunk, and "things would happen."

I felt sorry for them. My older brothers had warned me about those situations. What a sad way to lose such a precious, beautiful part of yourself — and to someone you hardly know. No wonder so many college students have sexually transmitted diseases! (More on that in Chapter 6.)

The Anti-Virginity Culture

The culture of cheap sex was everywhere on campus. In the event that anyone spontaneously felt like it, he or she could pick up a condom in one of the vending machines that also carried candy bars and chips in the dormitory lobbies. The school clinic widely publicized that birth control pills were available "in bulk," as well as "the Morning-After Pill." The Valentine's Day issue of the school newspaper was practically pornographic. Even the nonalcoholic dance club on campus was considered to be a "meat market."

What's a virgin to do?

In spite of all of these pressures, I was blessed to find many friends whose values were similar to my own. My next-door neighbor was a devout Christian who also had made the commitment to chastity. A few of the girls in concert choir and studio class were "secondary virgins." They had been sexually active, but since then, they had made the commitment not to have sex again until marriage. Several of the guys in the dorm were virgins and had made the commitment to chastity.

Of course, many of my friends were sexually active. I felt embarrassed and uncomfortable when they would tell me about their experiences. But I remained selfishly silent. Like a coward, I looked the other way, not saying a word as they continued in their destructive lifestyle. I made sure that I was making the best choice. I felt that my friends could take care of themselves. I wasn't a good friend.

It took another wake-up call in my life to break my silence, face the truth, and speak out for what was right. It was this traumatic, life-changing experience of a close friend that finally compelled me to be a voice for the voiceless and to stand with courage.

Allison's Story

During my freshman year I met a fantastic young woman who was brilliant, fun, inspiring, and strong in her faith. "Allison" was pre-law, and I knew that someday she would be an excellent judge. Her fiancé was an electrical engineering major and a really nice guy. This couple definitely had their act together.

When I ate lunch with them, I always felt a little bit embarrassed. Anyone who knows me knows that I have a rather large appetite, so my cafeteria tray would be filled with food. (Sometimes there would be so many plates on my tray that I could barely fit them all, and they hung off the edge!) My friend, on the other hand, would eat hardly anything. On her dinner plate were usually some carrot sticks, celery sticks, and maybe a dessert. But I didn't think very much of this. The next year, they got married; I sang at their wedding, and it was so beautiful! Everyone was filled with happiness!

One night several months later, I was studying in my dorm room when the phone rang. It was Allison's husband. I was very happy to hear his voice again — and I was looking forward to chatting with my friend.

I was completely unprepared for the news he had to share. Allison was in the hospital. "Oh, no," I thought. "A car accident."

But no — it was the unfathomable, the unthinkable. Allison was in the mental health ward. She had suffered a nervous breakdown.

I was shocked. Could this be true? Was this some kind of nightmare? My friend, my role model, my ideal . . . she had her life so together. She was the girl that I admired so much. How could it be that she was now in the psychiatric ward at Sacred Heart Hospital, just a few blocks away?

He asked me to visit her, and of course I promised to do so. But at that moment, I wanted nothing more than to get off the phone . . . I could hardly cope with my emotions. I heard in his voice that he wanted the same. The conversation ended quickly, with no questions and no explanations.

I couldn't understand it. Allison had seemed so happy just months ago at her wedding. This was a happy, talented, extremely intelligent, and virtuous young woman who was one of my closest friends. How could this have happened to her? How could I not have noticed that something was wrong? What could have caused this horrible sadness?

For a few days, I grappled with these questions that hung over my life like a dark cloud. There was little else I could think of. And yet, although I was thinking of Allison almost constantly, I selfishly didn't visit her.

I dreaded and feared that visit. I had never been to a psychiatric ward and had no idea what to expect. The thought of visiting one of my closest friends as a patient there was completely unbearable. It was bad enough to know that she was there — actually seeing her in one would be torture.

Then I realized how self-centered I was. Allison was there suffering, alone, while I was acting like a coward. I thought *I* was miserable from this news — imagine what she must be feeling! I couldn't procrastinate any longer. I left directly from my last class that day, with my backpack in tow, and climbed the hill to Sacred Heart Hospital.

The First Visit

I remember the first time I entered the hospital's fifth floor, which was the mental health unit. The elevator doors opened, and there was a locked security gate in front of me. As I stepped out of the elevator, I saw a nurse approach on the other side of the gate. I gave her my name and told her whom I was visiting. Her sad expression revealed to me that she knew Allison's story — my heart pounded as I tried to fathom what it might be.

As she led me to Allison's room, I felt like I was in some kind of an awful dream. "This isn't really happening," I thought. I tried to convince myself that it was all a mistake, that Allison wasn't really there, that this was my friend's idea of a joke.

And then I saw her. She was sitting forlornly on her bed in her white hospital gown, staring blankly into space. Her room was bare, without any cards, flowers, books, or even a TV. Only Allison and her empty stare.

She resembled the young woman I knew a few months ago. But there was a hopelessness, a lifelessness, and a deep sorrow that I had never seen in her before. Could this be my feisty, motivated, brilliant friend who was going to be the Chief Justice of the Supreme Court someday?

I didn't know what to say. I hugged her, and she seemed glad to see me, although she was very quiet. I tried to brighten her spirits by talking about everything and nothing . . . what was happening in the dorm, what our friends were up to, how my classes were going, what the latest activities on campus were. She took a languid interest in the news I had to share. She was silent and aloof, occasionally attempting a smile at some of my bad jokes and the silly stories of our friends.

I asked no questions. Although I was completely at a loss for what caused my friend's emotional collapse, I felt that if she wanted to, she would open up to me in her own time. And to be honest, I wasn't sure that I was ready to hear it.

The Second Visit — A Revelation

On my next visit, I brought Allison some flowers, a card, and a box of chocolates to cheer her up. The nurse took the candy from me, looking annoyed. "She can't have this," she said. Confused by her response, I followed her silently to Allison's room. As I passed by the rooms of other patients, I was again shocked and deeply distressed to see where my friend's life had taken her.

Allison was standing by the window, gazing outside at the beautiful fall colors. Eau Claire was always beautiful in the fall. We hugged, and I sat down next to her on the bed. Just like before, I did most of the talking while she seemed to half-listen, looking out the window.

I paused, studying her closely. Then I reached out for her hand, asking, "So how are you doing?"

"All right," she said, biting her lower lip. She told me a little about the place and kind of laughed as she confessed that she never thought she would be a patient in a psychiatric ward. She talked about a closet full of candy that was strictly monitored and opened for the patients once a day. She spoke about this with some excitement, like it was a highlight for her. She also scoffed a little as she described some of the other patients and the "dumb" activities they had to do each day. I smiled as she shared her experiences, grateful that she was opening up and talking.

Then she stopped suddenly, and pulled her knees up to her chest, looking lost in thought. "You know, I'd always thought about waiting until I was married to have sex." She turned away. I was surprised — why such a drastic change in topic? We'd never talked about this before. I remained silent, listening.

She continued, "A few years ago, my boyfriend and I were in a really passionate moment. And we decided we would just do it," she said. "I don't know . . . it just kind of happened."

She told me that she felt terribly guilty afterward, so much so that she tried to completely eliminate any physical contact between them. Then she realized that she was pregnant.

When his mother found out, she was furious. She insisted that Allison get an abortion, and offered to pay for it herself. "I didn't want to," Allison said, "but she said if I didn't, I couldn't marry her son. So I did."

Allison's eyes filled up with tears. "And every night since that awful day, I lie in bed, and I hear that little baby's voice crying out to me. That little baby wanted life. And I took it from him. And I hated myself so much for doing that, that I would try to escape from my life and the awful person that I was. And one way I thought I could escape was with food. I'd binge on Kit-Kats and candy bars, and sometimes I'd make myself throw up and sometimes I wouldn't. Finally, I just couldn't take it any more, I hated myself so much. And that's why — that's how I ended up here."

She started crying violently and hid her face in her hands. Her whole body shook as she wept. I put my arms around her, comforted her, tried to soothe her. But inside, I was numb. Was this some kind of a nightmare? I kept trying to tell myself, "This isn't really happening." But I knew that it was.

Soon after, the nurse came in and told me that it was time to go. Allison assured me that she was all right; she said that talking about it with me made her feel better.

I walked out of her room, changed forever.

My Ultimate Epiphany

I was in anguish. Another close friend had an eating disorder, and I never noticed. All this time, she was carrying this great burden, and I never knew. What kind of a friend was I?

I was angry at God. How could He allow such suffering to happen? I was angry at Allison's ex-boyfriend's mom. How could anyone be so horrible and insensitive as to force a girl to get an abortion? I was angry at her ex-boyfriend. How could he be such a wimp?

But most of all, I was angry at myself for not realizing that my friend needed help. If I had noticed her unhappiness or her eating problems, I could have gotten help for her, before her depression progressed to such an advanced state.

Allison and her experiences hung heavily on my heart. I brought her to God in prayer each night. I asked God to pick up the pieces of her life and make it all better, because I had no idea how anything could be salvaged from such sadness.

And I also prayed for myself. I realized that I was so blind and weak that I needed all the prayers I could get. I looked at myself in a new way — I saw myself for what I truly was. My "liberated" ideas no longer seemed quite so wise. My silence on chastity no longer appeared to be "open-minded" and "progressive." My hidden faith no longer was "free-thinking." I no longer subscribed to the idea that those who spoke out were trying to "force their ideas on others."

I was a *hypocrite* — and so self-absorbed that I didn't notice how very much my friends needed me.

My eyes were opened. I realized that every day, students on college campuses all over the country are suffering like Allison. Every day, guys and girls are taking risks without thinking, without knowing what the consequences could be. Every day, teens like Sarah think they are being "safe," when, in truth, they are throwing everything away! They are treating their precious sexuality as if it were something ordinary and worthless, like a Coke can instead of a chalice. And what was I doing about it? I was just standing by, taking good care that nothing happened to me while nonchalantly letting them risk their sexuality, their spirituality, and their futures.

Now, the message came to me loud and clear . . . *I am my brother's keeper!*

This phrase consumed me. My head learned it when I was in high school, after Sarah's experiences. But my heart and soul learned it now, and it possessed me for weeks. I was literally obsessed with this phrase. Whether I was walking around campus, singing during my voice lessons, studying in the library, or sleeping in my dorm room, I was haunted by this realization, and my lack of action. . . . *Your brother's blood cries out to me from the soil!* My friends, their shattered dreams, their suffering and deep emotional scars, irreversible consequences of actions that I might have been able to change. . . . *Truly, I say to you, as you did it not to one of the least of these, you did it not to me.*

How could I justify my silence? There was no justification. While my life continued in perfect form, unaffected by my cowardice, my friends' dreams were being shattered. "God, what have I done! How could I have allowed this to happen? I have been selfish and blind. While my friends have been suffering and making poor choices, I've said nothing, completely absorbed in my own life, and now my closest friends are suffering!"

I entered college thinking I was strong in my faith and ready to make an impact on others, but I was filled with pride and foolishness. I thought that I knew a great deal, when in truth I knew very little. It took a tragedy to make me see things clearly: If I wanted to make a difference, to be a positive influence on others and bring happiness to people's lives, then I needed to let Jesus take over full-time and become the central force in my life.

I asked what I needed to know. "God, what do You want of me? Guide me to do Your will, whatever it may be, and give me the strength to carry it out."

Allison's Conclusion

After two or three weeks, Allison was sent home from the hospital. Her husband watched over her lovingly and gave her many pets, since she loved animals. She doted on all of them, treating them like children. Occasionally we would chat on the phone, and she would tell me about their activities.

For five years, she and her husband tried to have a baby, "a little one," as Allison would say. They were longing to have a family. But Allison couldn't get pregnant, and her doctor told her that she probably never would. "I've reconciled myself to the fact that my little furry friends — these are my kids," she said to me one day, laughing sadly.

Then finally, Allison got pregnant! It was a high-risk pregnancy — both Allison's life and her baby's were at stake. I got together with Allison and her husband for lunch. She was tired but glad to be off the bed rest to which she had been confined for several weeks. Although it was hard, she and her husband were optimistic that they were going to have a healthy, happy baby. She was seeing a doctor who specialized in high-risk pregnancies, and he was becoming more positive that both Allison and her child would survive childbirth.

And then — wonderful news! Allison gave birth to a baby girl! Both mother and baby were relatively healthy, although Allison did suffer severe health problems for several months afterward. It was wonderful to see them together. Allison looked pale and tired, but I had never seen her glowing with such happiness before.

God had answered our prayers. Although Allison never fulfilled her dreams of becoming a judge, and this baby could never replace their first child, she and her husband had rediscovered happiness, after years of pain and regret.

God is so merciful and loving — He gave Allison the strength and forgiveness that she needed to move beyond the past. He welcomed her home with open arms. He blessed her with another child. He helped her and her husband to rebuild their relationship.

God empowered Allison to reconcile, repent, and heal.

A Graduation Manifesto

Although it was excruciating, something strange and wonderful happened inside of me during those last two years of college. I felt a longing to shed my fears and inadequacies — and to speak out for truth.

It was March of my senior year. I was drowning in graduate school applications, auditions, and financial aid forms, in addition to preparing for my senior recital. A personal "manifesto" was the last thing on my mind. But as I was eating lunch one Friday in the cafeteria, I saw a tabletop ad about a competition to be the commencement speaker at graduation.

Immediately, I knew that I had to enter. I wanted to be that speaker. I had a message for our class, and for everyone else who would attend the graduation as well.

That night, while my floor-mates were preparing for another wild weekend (taking showers, curling their hair, putting on makeup, deciding what to wear) I ran down to the twenty-four-hour computer lab in my dorm, eager to start writing. My head was swimming with ideas, so the speech came to me easily. I poured out my innermost thoughts, then headed up to my room for fine-tuning. While my peers were out at parties, bars, and dance clubs, I was pacing back and forth in my tiny dorm room, envisioning my generation's impact on the future, studying Kahlil Gibran's *The Prophet*, and praying to the Holy Spirit for inspiration. Writing, practicing, revising . . . this is how I would describe one of my most memorable Friday nights in college!

In the end, I came up with a speech that was like the blueprint for my life. It embodied the lessons I had learned from my college experiences, the wisdom that I had gained, and my dream for the future. It was certainly a speech for a graduation, and it fit into the time limit. But it was more than just a graduation address — it was my manifesto.

Shattering Expectations

I began by stating that our class was *not* going to fulfill the expectations of American society. (When I auditioned the piece in front of a distinguished group of UWEC faculty and staff, this created quite a stir. What kind of a commencement address was this?) But then I pointed out that society's expectations were that my generation would be lazy, apathetic, and selfish. I challenged my class to shatter these expectations by creating a new society where people gave without thought of return and by standing up for what was right, regardless of the consequences. We would seize this day, this moment, this opportunity in our lives to speak out for truth, and to create the kind of world that we had dreamed of.

"We have an opportunity," I emphasized, "to place our stamp on the world, to contribute to society, to find solutions to today's problems. And this is a chance we're not going to pass up."

My awakening had begun. I was no longer content to make excuses for my silence. I was no longer happy to take care of myself while I watched others make poor choices and throw away their dreams. I was no longer going to settle for sitting by and allowing the *real* truth to go unspoken. Now was the time to act.

I didn't have a vision of what I was going to do after graduation or five years down the line. I had no idea how I was going to carry out this manifesto, this challenge, this call to action. The only certainty in my life was that I was headed to Pittsburgh in the fall to pursue a Master of Music degree at Duquesne University. But I felt confident that God would show me the way.

I shared with my graduating class, "For whatever endeavor lies before each of us after graduation, our actions are going to change the lives of others. Our loved ones and our experiences here have given us the insight, courage, and ability to solve the problems of today's society. It's up to us. Our futures are an unwritten page, and today, we seize the pen to write our destiny."

It was time for me to take up my pen and write, to take up my cross and walk.

I did not know what that cross would be, but I was eager for it. God would unveil His plan to me when it was time. And I knew that in this plan, whatever it was, I would find difficulties and trials. But in this plan I also knew that I would discover my mission, my purpose, and my joy.

> And he said to all, "If any man would come after me, let him deny himself and take up his cross daily and follow me. For whoever would save his life will lose it; and whoever loses his life for my sake, he will save it."
>
> — Luke 9:23-24

6

The Suffering of My Generation

But Jesus turning to them said, "Daughters of Jerusalem, do not weep for me, but weep for yourselves and for your children. For behold, the days are coming when they will say, 'Blessed are the barren, and the wombs that never bore, and the breasts that never gave suck!' Then they will begin to say to the mountains, 'Fall on us'; and to the hills, 'Cover us.' For if they do this when the wood is green, what will happen when it is dry?"

— Luke 23:28-31

I began the master's program at Duquesne University with great anticipation, looking forward to growing in my art, knowledge, and spirituality. I knew that I would be quite busy with my studies and my work as a graduate assistant. Still, I was looking forward to studying at a Catholic university, and my apartment building was only a block from the lovely campus chapel.

Life as a graduate student was extremely hectic. In addition to my heavy workload for my classes, the voice faculty had many projects for me to do. Although it wasn't always the most stimulating or rewarding work, I knew that it had to be done, and if no one else wanted to do it, the task fell to me as the youngest graduate assistant. More interesting aspects of my job included writing down the staging for opera workshop scenes, organizing the repertoire lists for voice repertory classes, and, most of all, teaching private voice students and a class for freshmen music education majors.

Between my duties as a graduate assistant, my academic work, my extensive repertoire load for performance classes, and my adjustment to a new voice teacher, I had very little time for socializing. In addition, I was dating a young man who was working in the city, so most of my spare time was spent with him.

In spite of the extensive study, high expectations, and stress that came with pursuing a master's degree in a new city, my spiritual life flourished. Thanks to my boyfriend, I rediscovered spiritual reading, starting with a book that he gave me: *The Story of a Soul* by St. Thérèse of Lisieux.

This book deeply touched my life! It's impossible to describe how much I was moved by the words of this simple yet brilliant twenty-four-year-old. St. Thérèse brought Jesus to me in a completely new way and tremendously deepened my understanding of the Catholic faith and Jesus' passionate love for us. Through her, I learned that even the most minor activities of our lives are important. God looks upon the smallest aspects of our lives with great concern, even when they do not seem important to us at all. Tears flowed copiously the first time I made my way through the book, and I've taken it with me on all my travels ever since, reading it over and over, constantly inspired by Thérèse's heroic love and her words of wisdom and insight, which nourish my soul and touch my heart.

In graduate school, I returned to my practice of going to weekday Mass once or twice a week, just as I had in high school. Those quiet, introspective half-hours with Jesus were golden. The chapel had Mass three times a day, so I didn't have an excuse not to go. With the stress of politics in the music department and some discouraging setbacks in my singing, I had Jesus sustaining me every step of the way.

As I became immersed in my new life in Pittsburgh, the zeal that I had put into my graduation manifesto seemed like a distant memory. "Yes, it would be nice to take action, speak out for truth, and make the world a better place," I thought to myself almost every day. "But my life is so busy right now that I don't have time for those kinds of luxuries."

A Thirst for Truth

I wanted to forget the past and focus entirely on my singing and my work. But God wouldn't allow me to let the past go. There were things that I still needed to know. I was searching for answers.

The experiences of "Sarah" and "Allison" left me with a lot of questions — questions that couldn't be forgotten in the busyness of my life. Questions like: Why does society today encourage us to do things that come with such bad consequences? Why don't people ever talk to teens about the serious consequences that come with premarital sex, even "safe" sex? What about the emotional scars of sexual relationships that don't last? What does having an abortion or a baby out of wedlock mean for these girls' futures and their dreams? How come no one ever told us about the tough times that unmarried fathers go through? How can God let things like this happen? Are my friends just unlucky or is this how it is for a lot of teenagers?

This last question plagued me more than any other. Seeing two friends' shattered dreams, emotional scars, and lifelong regret was almost too much to bear. I had to know: Were their experiences unusual or are they just two of countless instances where premarital sex has devastated lives? Were my friends' experiences exceptions to the rule or representative of a suffering that silently encompassed an entire generation?

I hungered for the truth. But I was also afraid of what the truth might be.

I explored medical journals, books, magazines, and newspapers for comprehensive, unbiased information on the consequences of premarital sex, especially "safe" sex. The "facts" that I found seemed to conflict with one another. Most of what I read was opinion. I was searching for the full story — *the truth*, without any embellishments or exaggerations.

Frustrated, I eventually turned to the Internet, which I had always used only as a last resort in research. I knew that anything could be published on the Internet, whether or not it was true. I was skeptical that I would find anything useful.

I was completely wrong. During one of my searches on teen pregnancy, I discovered a fantastic resource for anyone seeking true, comprehensive information on the physical consequences of premarital sex. The website for the Medical Institute for Sexual Health (www.medinstitute.org) is a great find. It's a nonprofit organization of gynecologists, pediatricians, and child psychologists who are dedicated to promoting sexual health, particularly among teens. This site provides the most updated medical information available on all of the issues I was pondering, from teen pregnancy to sexually transmitted diseases to contraception . . . and the list goes on and on! I was impressed by the excellent sources that the Medical Institute uses — research from the most up-to-date studies published in highly respected medical journals such as the *New England Journal of Medicine*. I thought, "Surely these authoritative sources will provide the answers to my questions!"

The Truth Hurts

I was emotionally unprepared for what I found. I had spent so much time and energy looking for this information for many months, but after one afternoon of successful research, I wished that I had never pursued it.

It was far worse than I had ever imagined.

I was deeply disturbed by the statistics and information that I read. Could things really be this bad? I wanted to deny it, but with these authoritative sources, the information was impossible to refute. Here were the answers that I had been looking for. But they filled me with more questions than ever: If these things are true, why don't more people know? Why are these facts a secret? Why don't parents tell their children about these things? Or why hadn't our teachers told us? Why don't the members of the media inform the American public? Most of all, why does American society — which includes television networks, movies, magazines, newspapers, and even many school sex education programs — promote a big lie?

Over the next several months, I studied the articles and information cited on the Medical Institute's website. I found additional articles on the psychological and emotional impact of premarital sex. I did further research on teen pregnancy and sexually transmitted diseases like HPV, herpes, chlamydia, HIV, and genital warts (which will be explained later on in this chapter).

My friends' experiences weren't a fluke. They were just a typical sample of a much greater problem: Too many teens and young adults are suffering *devastating* — and *permanent* — consequences from choosing to participate in premarital sex.

The silent suffering of my generation was unveiled.

It's time for every teenager, young adult, parent, and teacher to know the truth. It isn't pretty — but facing reality is far better than choosing to be ignorant. In this case, what we don't know *can* hurt us.

The Truth About Teen Pregnancy in the United States

- One in five sexually active teen girls gets pregnant.
- About twenty-five hundred teens get pregnant every day, for a total of over nine hundred thousand each year.
- About fourteen to sixteen percent of couples that use condoms every time they have sex conceive in one year. This number increases for women under twenty-five.
- More than three hundred thousand teens get abortions every year (out of a total of 1.5 million surgical abortions annually).
- Only three out of ten girls who get pregnant before eighteen earn a high school diploma or its equivalent by age thirty.
- Sons of teenage mothers are 2.7 times more likely to spend time in prison than sons of women who delay childbearing into their twenties.

- Daughters of teen mothers are fifty percent more likely to have children out of wedlock than daughters of women who postpone childbearing into their twenties.
- Eighty percent of single mothers under age eighteen end up in poverty and on welfare.
- Single motherhood is the leading indicator of poverty in the United States.
- The United States has one of the highest teen pregnancy rates in the world among industrialized nations.

These statistics made me realize that Sarah and Allison's experiences weren't unusual at all. About nine hundred thousand other young women grapple with the trauma of teen pregnancy *every single year*. Nine hundred thousand dreams are shattered; nine hundred thousand lights may now be lost to the world. And every year, there are about three hundred thousand teens like Allison who get abortions. That's a lot of babies! And yet, it's only a portion of the astronomical number of abortions in the U.S. annually — 1.5 million!

I was surprised how many couples out there are like Sarah and her boyfriend who think that they are "safe" because they are using condoms. In school, we were told, "If you use condoms every time you have sex, you won't get pregnant." And yet, fourteen to sixteen percent of couples that always use condoms get pregnant in just one year! That's about *one out of six*. On TV and in the movies, they refer to condoms as being "safe." Why do they lie?

In an odd way, I realized that Sarah was lucky. She was among the fortunate thirty percent of girls who, in spite of getting pregnant before the age of eighteen, finish their high school education before age thirty. In fact, Sarah did better than that — she finished on time. And unlike eighty percent of other single teenage moms, she has never been on welfare. From these statistics, I realized that Sarah is a success story. And yet, look how difficult her life is.

How will those unwed teen moms without their high school diplomas survive? How will they support themselves and their children? How will they achieve their dreams?

Statistics show that "nonmarital pregnancy is the number one reason teenage girls go to the hospital."

This is very surprising. One would think that the main cause of teenage girls going to the hospital would be car accidents, eating disorders, depression, or alcohol poisoning. But it's not — it's *out-of-wedlock pregnancy*.

The Truth About Teen Pregnancy and Older Men

- Seventy percent of nonmarital teen pregnancies are fathered by men older than twenty.
- Studies show that when the mother is twelve or younger, the father averages twenty-two years of age.
- For mothers of junior high school age, the fathers average almost five years older.
- For mothers of high school age, the fathers average nearly four years older.

These disturbing statistics indicate that most teen pregnancies are fathered by men who are significantly older. What is a twenty-two-year-old doing with a twelve-year-old? That is disgusting! What are high school guys doing with middle school girls? Young women, I discourage you from dating anyone who is more than two years older than you before your high school graduation. Look at these statistics — they say it themselves. Avoiding older men just makes sense.

Parents and guardians need to be cognizant of whom their daughters and sons are spending time with, and what they are doing. If your parents or guardians ask you about your social life, don't get annoyed or defensive — just tell them the truth. They're not trying to be nosy or mean — they love you! You only get one shot at life. They want to make sure that you have the best life that you can, free of serious regrets.

Pregnancy outside of marriage is something that changes the lives of at least three people forever — the father, the mother, and the baby. Their lives will never be the same, and the consequences of an out-of-wedlock pregnancy are painful, difficult, and permanent.

But getting pregnant outside of marriage — or getting someone pregnant — isn't the worst thing that can happen to a person who has premarital sex. That's survivable, right? People usually live through that (except the baby sometimes)!

Here are more statistics that are a well-kept secret in today's society . . . things that you need to know.

The Truth About Sexually Transmitted Diseases in the United States

- More than sixty-five million people in the United States have been infected with an STD.
- Each day, there are over forty-two thousand cases of STDs, for a total of 15.3 million annually.
- Over eight thousand teens contract an STD every day, for a total of about three million teen infections each year.
- One out of four sexually active teens contracts a sexually transmitted disease.
- The United States has the highest rate of STDs of any industrialized nation in the world.
- There are more than twenty different STDs prevalent in the United States today.
- One in five Americans has been infected with a viral STD. (Bacterial diseases such as chlamydia, syphilis, and gonorrhea are not included in this statistic.)
- No medical cure has been found for a virus, even the common cold. Viral STDs (herpes, HPV, and HIV) are not curable.

- Two-thirds of bacterial sexually transmitted diseases occur in people under twenty-five years old.
- STDs can be passed through all types of intercourse.

These statistics are amazing — and horrifying. One out of four sexually active teens has an STD? This means that one out of four students at your school who is not a virgin is already infected with a sexually transmitted disease. You probably know four or more people in your school who are sexually active. Statistics say that at least one of them is infected. And every day the number of infected teens increases by eight thousand! That's a huge number! This morning, eight thousand kids woke up thinking, "It's not going to happen to me." These diseases don't discriminate based on what school a person attends, how high his or her GPA is, or where he or she lives — these diseases are rampant in big cities, small towns, and mid-sized suburbs.

In addition, the fact that STDs can be passed through *all types* of intercourse is significant. This is the difference between abstinence and chastity. Remember that chastity is a conscious choice to embrace purity. It doesn't ask, "How much can I do and still technically be called a virgin?" That's not a call to action — that's a passive, lukewarm, wimpy approach. Rather, chastity asks, "How much can I save for my future spouse and for God?"

Let's look at some of these sexually transmitted diseases in a little more detail.

Chlamydia

- Chlamydia is the most common STD among teens in the United States.
- There are about three million to four million cases of chlamydia in the U.S. each year.
- Chlamydia is the leading cause of infertility among women.
- Chlamydia causes Pelvic Inflammatory Disease (PID), which creates scar tissue in the uterus.

- Adolescents are more susceptible to sexually transmitted diseases because their bodies are still developing. A sexually active fifteen-year-old has an estimated one-in-eight chance of getting PID, whereas a twenty-four-year-old's chances of getting PID are one in eighty.
- In four out of five cases of chlamydia, there are no symptoms. When a person is infected with an STD but is not experiencing symptoms, that person usually does not know that he or she is infected.
- If a young woman contracts chlamydia and it goes untreated, it often leads to infertility, especially if she contracts it three or more times, even from the same partner. Sometimes it is referred to as the "silent sterilizer."
- Chlamydia is a bacterial infection. If a person is aware that he or she has this disease, it can be cured with antibiotics.
- *There is no conclusive evidence that condoms provide any protection against chlamydia.*

Genital Herpes

- One out of five Americans over age eleven has genital herpes.
- Herpes is a virus, not a bacterial infection. (If a person contracts this disease once, he or she will have this disease for a lifetime and infect everyone the individual has sex with.)
- This disease causes an itchy and painful rash similar to hives on the genital area or wherever there has been skin contact with an infected area.
- Outbreaks of this rash can be limited to every three to four months, with the consistent, lifetime use of an expensive antibiotic.
- Herpes can be transmitted between outbreaks, even if one doesn't see a rash.
- If a child is born during a mother's outbreak of herpes, the child can contract this disease and even die from it.

- Herpes is passed through skin-to-skin contact. *There is no conclusive evidence that condoms provide any protection against this disease.*

HPV (Human Papilloma Virus)

- HPV is the most common STD in the United States — *over five million people are infected each year.*
- Forty percent of sexually active singles have HPV, and many people don't know that they are infected.
- Strains of this disease can cause warts on the genital area, which remain with a person throughout his or her life and must be removed surgically on a regular basis.
- HPV causes over ninety eight percent of cervical cancer cases.
- HPV also causes cancer of the penis, uterus, and vulva.
- Complications resulting from HPV cause about five thousand deaths every year.
- HPV is a virus. Those contracting this disease once will have it for the rest of their lives and pass it on to everyone they have sex with.
- A woman's risk of contracting HPV increases *tenfold* with each new partner.
- More than half of sexually active single women will catch HPV if they continue sexual activity for over three years.
- HPV is passed through skin-to-skin contact. *There is no evidence that condoms provide any protection against this disease.*

HIV (Human Immunodeficiency Virus)

- Nine hundred thousand living Americans are infected with HIV.
- The majority of Americans who are infected with HIV don't realize that they have this disease.
- About sixty-five thousand Americans contract HIV each year.

- HIV can appear in the bloodstream up to two years after a person has contracted it.
- HIV is a deadly disease whose effect can be postponed with the use of many expensive and powerful antibiotics on a daily basis for the rest of a person's life.
- HIV is a virus. If a person contracts this disease once, he or she will have it for a lifetime, and pass it on to any person that the individual has sex with.
- *Condoms are most effective against HIV in comparison with other STDs but still have a fifteen percent failure rate against this virus.*

Wow! These diseases are serious — cancer, infertility, genital warts, even death. These are things that will be with a person forever and impact extremely important parts of a person's life.

Guys, imagine that you have found the woman of your dreams. She is kind, intelligent, spiritual, strong, honest, and a lot of fun to be with. The two of you are so in love! You know that this is the person you want to spend the rest of your life with! You have a beautiful diamond ring. You get down on one knee, and ask, "Will you marry me?"

And then you have to say, "By the way, I have genital warts."

Wouldn't that be awful? It might be funny to laugh at the idea, but the reality of that kind of a situation is horrible. That's how it is for millions of people in our country today.

Is it worth it to take the risk?

'Safe' Sex

- Fourteen to sixteen percent of couples who use condoms every time they have sex get pregnant in one year.
- Condoms provide little if any protection against a variety of STDs passed through skin-to-skin contact, including the most common STD in the U.S., HPV.
- Fifty-three percent of unintended pregnancies occur in women using birth control.

- Two to four percent of condoms slip or break during use.
- Even with all their failures, condoms are the most effective form of protection against STDs.

What is this? For the past two decades, sex education programs in this country have taught us that condoms are "safe." How many times have we heard on TV, the radio, in movies, in magazines, newspaper articles, and even in health class, "If you use condoms every time, you won't get pregnant"?

I wish it were that simple.

As one expert concluded, "Condoms are widely promoted for preventing sexually transmitted disease, with an implicit message that a properly used condom will ensure that you are safe from STDs. A literature review shows that little solid evidence supports this belief."

The truth was staring me in the face: The "safe sex" myth that is promoted by the media and schools across the country is a lie. Abstinence is the only one hundred percent effective method. Millions of young people in my generation are suffering the devastating and permanent impact of sexually transmitted diseases, pregnancy outside of marriage, and painful emotional scars from having sex too early . . . from believing a lie.

Awakened to the truth, I realized that I couldn't remain silent any longer.

The time had come for me to stand with courage.

––––––––––

The medical and statistical information in this chapter was provided by the following sources:

Alan Guttmacher Institute. *Facts in Brief: Contraceptive Use*, 2000.

Alan Guttmacher Institute. *Facts in Brief: Sexually Transmitted Diseases in the United States*, 1993.

Alan Guttmacher Institute. *Facts in Brief: Teen Sex and Pregnancy*, September 1999.

Alan Guttmacher Institute. *Facts in Brief: Teen Sex and Pregnancy*, July 1996.

Alan Guttmacher Institute. *Sex and America's Teenagers*, 1994.

Alan Guttmacher Institute. *Teenage Pregnancy: Overall Trends and State-by-State Information*, 1999.

American Social Health Association and Kaiser Family Foundation. *Sexually Transmitted Diseases in America: How Many Cases and at What Cost?* December 1998.

Cates, W., Jr., and Stone, K. M. "Family Planning, Sexually Transmitted Diseases and Contraceptive Choice: A Literature Update — Part 1." *Family Planning Perspectives*, 1992; 24(2):75-84.

Centers for Disease Control and Prevention. "Sexually Transmitted Disease Surveillance 1995." *Mortality and Morbidity Weekly Report*, September 1996.

Centers for Disease Control and Prevention. *Prevention of Genital HPV Infection and Sequelae: Report of an External Consultants' Meeting*. Department of Health and Human Services, December 1999.

Challenge Task Force on Chastity. *A Challenge for the New Millennium*, 1999.

Dietrich, J. *AIDS: Fact vs. Fiction*. Focus on the Family, 1994.

Fu, H., Darroch, J. E., Haas, T., and Ranjit, N. "Contraceptive Failure Rates: New Estimates from the 1995 National Survey of Family Growth." *Family Planning Perspectives*, 1999; 31:56-63.

Eng, T., and Butler, W. T., eds. Institute of Medicine. *The Hidden Epidemic — Confronting Sexually Transmitted Disease*. Washington, D.C.: National Academy, 1997.

Jamison, J., et al. "Spectrum of Genital Human Papillomavirus Infection in a Female Adolescent Population." *Sexually Transmitted Diseases*, 1999; 11(4), 236-243.

Jones, E. F., and Forrest, J. D. "Contraceptive Failure Rates based on the 1988 NSFG." *Family Planning Perspectives*, 1999; 24(1), 12-19.

Kreiss, J., et al. "Human Immunodeficiency Virus, Human Papillomavirus, and Cervical Intraepithelial Neoplasia in Nairobi Prostitutes." *Sexually Transmitted Diseases*, 1992; 19(1), 54–59.

McIlhaney, J. S., Jr. *Sex: What You Don't Know Can Kill You.* Grand Rapids, Michigan: Baker, 1997.

Medical Institute for Sexual Health. *Condom Sense: Has the Truth Been Covered Up?* 1998.

Mishell, D. R.. "Contraception." *New England Journal of Medicine*, 1989; 320(12), 777–787.

Morris, B. "How Safe are Safes? Efficacy and Effectiveness of Condoms in Preventing STDs." *Canadian Family Physician*, 1993; 39, 819–827.

National Institute of Allergy and Infectious Diseases, National Institutes of Health. *Fact Sheet: An Introduction to Sexually Transmitted Diseases*, July 1999, and *Fact Sheet: Sexually Transmitted Diseases Statistics*, December 1998. Department of Health and Human Services.

National Institutes of Health, April 1-3, 1996. *Cervical Cancer: NIH Consensus Development Statement.* Online, 43(1), 1–30.

National Institutes of Health. *Scientific Evidence of Condom Effectiveness for Sexually Transmitted Disease (STD) Prevention*, July 2001.

Warner, D. I., and Hatcher, R. A. "Male Condoms." *Contraceptive Technology*, 17th ed. New York: Irvington Publishers, 1998.

Weller, S. C. "A Meta-analysis of Condom Effectiveness in Reducing Sexually Transmitted HIV," *Social Science and Medicine*, 1993; 36(12), 1635–1644.

7

A Call to Witness

You did not choose me, but I chose you and appointed you that you should go and bear fruit.

— John 15:16

It makes God sad to witness the results of people's poor choices — so many dreams lost, so many gifts misused, so much potential unfulfilled. That's why God needs us to witness to Him in the world so that more people can experience the joy of following His ways. My friend, God has given you a mission that only you can accomplish, a witness that only you can bring to the world! And this mission is *crucial!* There are people out there whose hearts need to be touched in a way that only you can touch them. They need to experience compassion, and love, and guidance, and wisdom — and you're the one who must bring this into their lives! Your mission will probably be tough, but it will also be awesome amounts of fun! *God needs you so much! The world needs you so much!*

It's easy to think, "Come on! I'm such a flawed person — how can God be calling me?" St. Thérèse, the Little Flower, once wrote, "God doesn't call those who are worthy, but those whom He wishes to call." I see this in my own life. I'm not the most devout or prayerful young woman, and I'm definitely not the most courageous. But God looked at me, with all of my weaknesses and imperfections, and decided to bless my life with a very fun-filled and exciting mission — to be a *rebel for truth* in today's world, speaking out for chastity.

I knew the positive reasons to put chastity into action, because I live them each day. I'm growing in self-respect . . . love

. . . courage . . . integrity . . . strength . . . purity . . . inner peace . . . respect and appreciation for other people. I have a greater understanding of what's really important in romantic relationships. I have a fun-dating life. I'm preparing for a happy, fulfilling marriage. I'm achieving my goals and dreams. I feel good because I'm living a life based on truth. Most of all, I'm staying on track for the awesome plan that God has for my life, whatever it might be.

But when it came to actually speaking about chastity, I was terrified! I definitely didn't respond the way that Mary did to the angel, "I am the handmaid of the Lord; let it be to me according to your word"(Luke 1:38). I was reluctant, overwhelmed, and afraid. The more informed I became about the widespread and devastating consequences of premarital sex, the more hopeless I felt.

"What can one person do about it anyway?" I wondered. "The problem is enormous. I'm already overwhelmed with my classes and work. I don't have the time to do this. Even if I did, it's way out of my control."

But a voice in my heart kept calling me to do more. *It was a call to action!* It was telling me to be "a voice in the wilderness," to speak out for truth, to stand with courage.

Lots of Baggage

Many things held me back from speaking about chastity. Although I had done a fair amount of public speaking on a variety of topics, this subject was completely out of my reach. In fact, I couldn't even say the word "sex" without feeling embarrassed and stuttering a little! How was I supposed to get up and talk about it in front of a group of teens?

Another major problem: I was almost as uncomfortable saying the word "virgin."

How could I speak about abstinence without saying "sex" or "virgin"? It was impossible.

Then I remembered the words of "Walk a Little Slower, My Friend," the song that originally inspired me to make the commitment to chastity.

Keep aiming high . . .
Reach for the sky,
And do your best to make things happen.

Think it over, my friend.
Don't pass it by or let it slip away.
Grab your chance and take it —
Life is only what you make it.
Start here and now to live it, every day.

Wasn't this the creed that I once lived by? To live life to the fullest . . . to keep trying and always do my best . . . to be open to every opportunity that comes my way?

And yet, how many opportunities had I allowed to "slip away" in the past several years? Was I now going to allow fear of failure to prevent me from trying? Or was I going to "reach for the sky" and do my best to "make things happen"?

The time had come for me to put my graduation manifesto into action and "find solutions to today's problems." I longed to "seize the pen to write my destiny," "to make a difference," "to change people's lives in a positive way" so that fewer teens and young adults suffer from destructive choices. I was no longer willing to stand by and watch others make the same mistakes that my friends had made. I had to act!

But the question was: How?

Searching for My Voice

My first challenge came much sooner than I expected. One of my private voice students was an eighteen-year-old high school graduate who was a full-time waitress in downtown Pittsburgh.

After dating a young man for a few months, she casually mentioned during her singing lesson that he had invited her to move into his apartment, and she was thinking about doing it.

I was shocked, but I had the clarity of mind to think, "Here's your chance to make a difference, to help this young woman make a good choice."

I tried to express disapproval to her in a nice way, using feel-good phrases that I had heard before. "Are you sure you're ready for that? What if it doesn't work out? You don't need to do that. You're too good for that. If he loved you, he wouldn't ask you to do that."

She seemed to be amused by my fluffy advice. I could tell that my arguments sounded weak and a little prudish to her. Even though I was only three years older, I think that she thought I was "out of touch" with her lifestyle. A couple of weeks later, she moved in with him, and stopped studying voice shortly thereafter.

I was ashamed of myself. My first trial was a huge failure! I not only came off as being judgmental, but I couldn't even articulate some important reasons for her to consider not moving in with him. "Why couldn't I just tell it like it is?" I thought in frustration. I had been too embarrassed to talk about the real, concrete reasons for chastity — from pregnancy and STDs to spirituality, a better relationship, a healthy sense of self-respect, and future goals. I felt discouraged. "Maybe it would have been better if I hadn't said anything," I thought.

My idea of speaking to teens about chastity now seemed to be more unrealistic than ever. "Jesus, there must be some other way," I prayed. "Show me Your way."

Nourishing the Seed

God always answers our prayers, but not always in the way that we have in mind. He brought three opportunities into my path that combined to create a powerful — and very unexpected — vehicle for my mission. Little did I know that these three simple events would point the way to a very unexpected mission.

June 26, 1999 — You dream about a moment like this, but it never compares to the reality! Thank You, God!

This is my nerdy picture from freshman year of high school. There's hope for everyone! (If you ever feel bad about yourself, look at this picture!)

What a transformation! Here I am just seven months later. I'm wearing one of my costumes from our school musical *My Fair Lady*.

This is my senior picture from high school,
which is pretty close to what I look like today.
Suspenders used to be "in" — really!

After four years of hard work, graduation rocks! Here I am delivering the commencement address for the Class of 1996 at the University of Wisconsin-Eau Claire, "Generation X — Shattering Expectations!" (The distinguished professor behind me doesn't look quite as excited as I was.)

Another milestone in my life — my Master of Music degree from Duquesne University. With me are my mom and dad, who are always around for the major events in my life, especially graduations. They try to keep me out of trouble!

My siblings and I take time out from fooling around for a quick picture. Here are John, Elizabeth, Tom, and my sister-in-law Kim.

Talk about the pressure being on! But for some reason, I felt pretty cool during the Top Five interview at the Miss Wisconsin Pageant. Fellow contestants Michelle Kojis and Kristen Tielens await their turns.

It was the experience of a lifetime — performing my talent piece at the Miss America Pageant. I sang the Italian aria "Il Bacio," meaning "The Kiss."

Winning the talent competition at Miss America was awesome! After Heather and I took the runway, our fellow contestants did the traditional "pageant rush," with hugs and congratulations.

The evening wear competition at Miss America was full of surprises. This picture was taken before the unexpected happened! (See Chapter 10 for details.)

Here I am with Nana backstage at Miss America. There was a "behind the scenes" tour for contestants' families during a rehearsal. Families and friends wear buttons with their contestants' pictures on them, for moral support.

Making Top Ten at Miss America was incredibly exciting! I'm fifth from the left. (The winner, Heather French, is second from the right.)

My passion is speaking to teens across the country.

These seniors from Rockford Lutheran High School were almost too enthusiastic about my talk — they pushed classmates out of the way to volunteer! They also look pretty proud of themselves in their chastity T-shirts.

This is my ultimate role model, Elayne Bennett, the founder of Best Friends and Best Men. She is also a wonderful wife and mother . . . and looks great in the Miss Wisconsin crown!

Over four thousand girls around the country make the Best Friends commitments to postpone sex, reject drugs and alcohol, and focus on their educational and career goals. And they support one another in these commitments — awesome! (This is a group of Best Friends girls from Milwaukee.)

Signing shirts, hats, and sneakers after my talks was another fun part of the job.

This young man isn't afraid to show others that he has high standards! Definitely "virgin and studly!"

This good-looking group was in the studio audience when I was on *Life on the Rock*. I loved hanging out with them in the "coffeehouse" after the show.

This is Jeff Cavins, the super-cool host of *Life on the Rock*. He wouldn't put on the crown during the show, but I managed to get it on his head for a quick picture afterward!

Here are a few of the Diamond Girls from the Milwaukee Best Friends chapter. They're high schoolers who are staying true to their Best Friends commitments. Their inner beauty shines through!

My sister, Elizabeth, and her husband, David, had a beautiful wedding — the beginning of a great marriage!

Chastity rocks! And so do these youth camps across the country! This was taken at the Diocese of Erie's Journey to Emmaus 2001, where I spoke about "Body Beautiful: The Body of Christ." Check out the banner behind me — it looks almost like my shadow! Pretty funny!

A Sign

One day, as I came out of a practice room in the Duquesne music building, I saw a sign posted to recruit contestants for the Miss Southwestern Pennsylvania Pageant, a preliminary to Miss Pennsylvania and Miss America. I had done a Miss America local pageant once before, when I was seventeen, and won. I had even been in the Top Ten at Miss Wisconsin that year. But that seemed like such a long time ago, and I had vowed that I'd never do another pageant again.

So why did that sign catch my eye every time I walked by?

Then I was struck by a thought. The Miss America program's emphasis on community service could be a great way to reach teens about chastity. In the program, each contestant promotes a "platform," an issue that is very important to her. If she wins the pageant, whether she becomes Miss Pittsburgh, Miss Pennsylvania, or Miss America, her year of service is dedicated to her chosen platform. Platforms of previous Miss Americas included literacy, overcoming disabilities, diabetes, and AIDS awareness.

"This is the answer!" I thought. "Abstinence could be my platform, which would give this issue a lot of publicity. Wouldn't it be great if Miss Pennsylvania promoted abstinence? Or even Miss America? It would be in the papers and on the radio, and students would hear about it! People could be touched by that."

I contacted the director of the Miss Southwestern Pennsylvania Pageant. He told me that I wasn't eligible to compete, because I hadn't yet been a full-time student in Pennsylvania for six months. However, he was hosting another local pageant a few months later, and by that time, I would fulfill the residency requirement.

Knowing the importance of the platform in the Miss America program, I was excited about bringing abstinence into the pageant culture. I began to enthusiastically brainstorm ways to promote abstinence — preferably without my having to say the words "sex" or "virgin."

I know that this sounds ridiculous! How can anyone speak effectively about chastity without being comfortable and open enough to say those words? But I was intimidated. I knew my limitations.

Little did I know that God would lift me above my narrow horizons and that His vision was far greater than my own!

A Show

Several months later, shortly after I won a local preliminary for Miss Pennsylvania, God brought another experience into my life that would point the way. After going out with friends one weekend night, I casually turned on EWTN, the global Catholic TV network, as I was getting ready for bed.

I couldn't believe it! There was a woman on TV speaking about abstinence to teens! I had never heard of anyone speaking on this issue before. This was too timely to be a coincidence.

The students were deeply impacted by her message. Although she was about fifteen years older than I (she was also married with a family), she had a great connection with the students. Her firm and confident delivery, her mastery of medical facts, and her experiences as a counselor at a crisis pregnancy center were compelling.

I also was impressed by the way that she organized her presentation, dividing it into sections based on the consequences of premarital sex. She gave me a model to begin with, and something to strive for. At the end of the program, I learned that her name was Pam Stenzel. I had a new hero. And I renewed my determination to overcome my insecurities so that I could start being part of a solution to the sad epidemic of the culture of death — rather than just feeling overwhelmed and doing nothing.

An Article

About a week later, a third opportunity was brought into my life. My mother mailed me an article that she had read in *Reader's Digest*. It was about a national character-building program for girls in grades four through twelve called Best Friends. The program was founded in 1987 by Elayne Bennett in Washington, D.C., and there were over twenty sites across the country, mostly in urban public school systems. The participants meet weekly to support one another in abstaining from sex, drugs, alcohol, and tobacco, while striving for their educational and career goals. Each girl also meets individually on a weekly basis with a mentor who gives her guidance and encouragement to deal with problems the girl is facing, while inspiring her to be the best that she can be. The program has already met with tremendous success. In the District of Columbia, the teen pregnancy rate was twenty-six percent. Among Best Friends girls, though, it was just one percent.

The curriculum has a very positive, upbeat approach. Rather than going with a "just say no" type of philosophy, it emphasizes that abstinence from sex, drugs, and alcohol is truly saying *"yes"* to the rest of your life! As I said to the Best Friends girls years later as Miss Wisconsin, "Every time you say no to sex outside of marriage . . . every time you say no to drugs and alcohol use and violence . . . you're saying *yes* to your future, *yes* to your dreams, *yes* to making a difference in the world."

This is the Best Friends message, and thousands of young women all over the country put it into action every single year! Some of these girls come from extremely difficult family situations. One or both of their parents might be struggling with addictions or abusive behavior. Many don't have parents, and many live on welfare. But these amazing young ladies continue to hope, dream, and choose the best. The program has a one hundred percent high school graduation rate, and many of the participants go on to college and graduate school.

"This is it!" I thought as I read the article. "This is what life is really all about!" What could be more meaningful than helping other people to rise above tough situations in their lives and achieve their dreams?

Researching Best Friends on the Internet, I was amazed by the number of terrific articles written about this program in magazines and newspapers across the country. Their success was inspiring, and their message was exactly what I believed and lived out. It seemed too much of a coincidence that this article had come to me at this point in my life. It was obvious that Jesus had placed this in my path!

"There must be something I can do for them," I thought. "It would be so wonderful to encourage these young women and help them to stick to their convictions and achieve their dreams."

I contacted the national headquarters in Washington, D.C., and found out that there were Best Friends chapters in both Milwaukee and Pittsburgh! What a joy! After interviewing with each program director, I was invited to be a role model speaker for the girls at both sites.

A sign, a show, an article . . . I had asked for a way to speak to teens about chastity. I had asked for direction. I thought I'd get the answer in a dramatic way, like a lightning bolt would hit me, or a statue would talk to me, or I'd receive some mysterious letter in the mail. These three everyday events seemed so simple, so random.

And yet, how random were they? I didn't realize it at the time, but these "everyday" events were the unexpected answer to my prayers. My journey had moved to a new level. The adventure had begun.

8

Trial by Fire

And I will put this third into the fire,
    and refine them as one refines silver,
    and test them as gold is tested.
They will call on my name,
    and I will answer them.
I will say, "They are my people";
    and they will say, "The LORD is my God."

— ZECHARIAH 13:9

In this you rejoice, though now for a little while you may have to suffer various trials, so that the genuineness of your faith, more precious than gold which though perishable is tested by fire, may redound to praise and glory and honor at the revelation of Jesus Christ.

— 1 PETER 1:6-7

Blessed is the man who endures trial, for when he has stood the test he will receive the crown of life which God has promised to those who love him.

— JAMES 1:12

Little did I realize that these three elements — a sign, a show, and an article — would point the way to my mission, which would eventually lead to my becoming Miss Wisconsin. But this was no easy rise to success. It was a three-year "trial by fire" filled with failures and disappointments before I finally won a state title.

Feeling Like a Failure?

We all experience failure from time to time. It's a part of life — sometimes we succeed, and sometimes we fail. But have you ever felt that your life is just one failure after the next? Or worse, have you ever felt that you yourself are a failure?

In today's world, talking about your failures is viewed as being very "politically incorrect." Our society sees it as humiliating and even downright shameful for someone to admit she's failed, that something was difficult for her, or that she has faced a lot of disappointment and defeat. It's much easier and more glamorous to say, "I won on my first try!" "I always get it right!" or, "I've never been defeated!"

But how much more strength and courage does it take for us to be honest and admit that we've experienced failure? How much more character does it take to taste the bitterness of defeat and to come back and try again? This is the "trial by fire" that "refines" us into better people and makes us stronger!

As I look back on my journey to the crown, I see that the many failures I faced competing in pageants were crucial in preparing me to for the challenges that awaited me when I finally won. The lessons I learned and the understanding I gained from these failures built a solid and meaningful foundation — "tiny, hard-won blocks of failure," as Jamie Clarke said when he described how his failed attempts to climb Mount Everest helped him make it to the top. These failures became my strength as I went on to greater challenges, not only in pageants, but in *life!*

I hope that as you read this, you'll think about how your own failures have helped make you a stronger, better person. Perhaps you've had some disappointments, setbacks, and failures along your journey. Maybe there is one in particular that weighs on your heart heavily — a race that you lost, a class that you failed, a role that you auditioned for and didn't get. If so, read on! Because this chapter isn't only about my "trial by fire" — it's about yours.

God 'Saves Us From Ourselves'!

Although I felt the certainty of God's call to be "a voice in the wilderness" by speaking out for chastity, God knew that this calling would be very difficult for me. He recognized that it was far beyond my abilities at that point in my life; I wasn't ready to take on the difficulties that I would encounter in bringing this message to the world. In order to prepare me, God allowed me to experience many setbacks and discouragements on my journey. He used these to strengthen me, developing my heart, soul, and mind for the mission ahead.

God does this in everyone's life! As my sister says, "Man makes plans, and God laughs." For example, let's say that you have a dream and pray very hard for it. But God knows that this dream wouldn't be good for you in the long run or make you happy. So your dream goes unfulfilled. Does this mean that God wasn't listening? No way! Instead, He has something even better in store for you! God "saved you from yourself" — He didn't give you what you wanted, because He's going to give you something much better!

It's easy to see this in my own life. For many years, one of my dreams has been to become a professional opera singer. This dream hasn't yet come true — but that doesn't mean that it never will. God simply had other plans for me along the way, including becoming Miss Wisconsin, working with teens, and writing this book. These things have brought me so much joy and happiness! These things also have made me a better person — stronger, more compassionate, less focused on myself, and more focused on others. By not fulfilling my dream, my life is richer and more meaningful than I ever could have imagined! God's dream was far better than my plans. Life is full of wonderful surprises.

Suffering — Something Good?

At times, though, the surprises aren't so wonderful. Sometimes terrible things occur for seemingly no reason at all. There are a lot of unfair and evil things that happen in the world, things that seem to be expressly against God's will. Sometimes we want to cry out, "God, why do You allow things like this to happen?"

It's at these times of trial when our faith has to be the strongest. This is the real "trial by fire." In your life and in mine, even when things look like they can't get any worse, we must remember that God is still in charge! He takes bad situations and transforms them into opportunities for blessings and grace. If we can "stand strong" with God during these tough times, He'll make us stronger and more prepared to triumph later on, when the stakes are highest.

We must not forget something very important: Our suffering has meaning. When things don't work out the way you want or something terrible happens, you're actually sharing in Jesus' suffering on the Cross. St. Paul tells us that our sufferings make up for what is lacking in the Body of Christ, the Church. So when you offer your sadness and suffering up to God, you're actually participating in the redemptive work of Jesus! He really knows what it's like to suffer, because He made the greatest sacrifice ever offered — He gave Himself completely and died for our sins so that you and I could be saved.

God always sees your suffering, even when you feel completely alone. He will reward you for your sacrifice. "For as we share abundantly in Christ's sufferings, so through Christ we share abundantly in comfort too" (2 Corinthians 1:5).

God Is There for You!

My friend, please remember that no matter how bad things get, *God is always there for you!* He is with you, and is longing to help you — all you have to do is ask! He wants to carry you through those tough times in your life. That reminds me of one of my favorite stories, *Footprints*, by an unknown author.

One night, a man had a dream. He dreamed that he was walking along the beach with the Lord. Across the sky flashed scenes from his life. For each scene, he noticed two sets of footprints in the sand: one belonging to him, and the other to the Lord.

When the last scene of his life flashed before him, he looked back at the footprints in the sand. He noticed that many times along the path of his life there was only one set of footprints. He also noticed that it happened at the very lowest and saddest times in his life. This really bothered him and he questioned the Lord about it.

"Lord, you said that once I decided to follow you, you'd walk with me all the way. But I noticed that during the most troublesome times in my life, there is only one set of footprints. I don't understand why when I needed you most you would leave me."

The Lord replied, "My precious, precious child, I love you and I would never leave you. During your times of trial and suffering, when you see only one set of footprints, it was then that I carried you."

God never abandons us or forgets about us, even when it feels like He has. As I endured difficulties and discouragements on my journey to win a state title in the Miss America program, I sometimes felt that God had forgotten about me. But when I look back, I realize that, like the man in the story above, during these many trials the Lord carried me every step of the way.

Trial Number One — First Time at Miss Pennsylvania

After winning the local title of Miss Three Rivers (for Pittsburgh's Allegheny, Monongahela, and Ohio rivers), I headed into the Miss Pennsylvania Pageant with confidence that out of the twenty-four contestants, I would be a main contender for the title. I thought that I was prepared to win. (I was wrong!)

Although I had done a great deal of research on abstinence, I hadn't done any other preparation for the interview portion of competition, which is actually the most important part. The judges at the Miss Three Rivers Pageant told me that they were "very impressed" with the way that I had handled their questions during the interview and that they "didn't believe that this platform would hold me back, as it had for other contestants." The idea that the abstinence platform might make things harder for me in competition had never crossed my mind. But I was pleased with what they said and felt I didn't need to do any other preparation for the interview portion.

Negativity

Unfortunately, I had given in to negative thinking for several months, feeling discouraged about my singing, my appearance, and even the person that I was. Instead of looking outward at the world and thinking about how I could make it a better place, I was focused on looking inward, finding things wrong with myself.

Negative thinking — thoughts like, "I'm not good at anything," "I'm so ugly," or "I'm sure I'll mess up again because I always do" — is very harmful. It causes a person to become passive rather than active, existing rather than living, reacting to life rather than taking charge. It robs individuals of their ability to love others and bringing their unique light to the world! If I dislike myself, how can I love — or even like — other people?

My lack of interview preparation and my negative thinking made the Miss Pennsylvania competition week one of the worst weeks of my life. I was so anxious that I actually broke out in hives on Monday morning, the first day of rehearsals! By Thursday, when we had our interviews and the first night of competition, I had such a terrible sore throat that I was unable to talk and swallowing was painful. I croaked my way through the interview, convinced that the judges didn't like me. I was so sick that the doctor tested me for mono and told me sadly, "It would take a miracle for you to be able to sing tomorrow night."

The next day, I felt slightly better, and I kept praying that God would heal my voice so that I could perform my talent in the competition. He answered my prayers — about an hour before the pageant, my throat started to feel better, and I was able to sing! I even won the preliminary talent competition that night. I was overjoyed. This was forty percent of the total score! It put my mind at ease. "The judges must really like me!" I thought.

Perhaps this made the final night all the more devastating. In spite of my talent win, I was not named among the Top Ten contestants with the highest preliminary scores, who would go on to compete for the title of Miss Pennsylvania.

I felt terrible about my poor showing. My family had traveled from all over the country to support me in this pageant, with the expectation that I would be among the top contenders. After all, I had made the Top Ten at Miss Wisconsin when I was only eighteen years old. But at twenty-two, with a college degree and an opera apprenticeship in Austria under my belt, I couldn't even equal that performance.

"I was better four years ago than I am now!" I thought.

Spiritual Immaturity

It's hard not to take pageant defeats personally. In sports, if another person runs faster, or throws farther, or jumps higher, that person wins. In music, if another person plays better or sings more beautifully, he or she gets the part. But in pageants, you're judged on personal qualities — talent, intelligence, personality, speaking ability, level of accomplishment, elegance, and even looks. So when you lose, it's not just because someone ran faster or played better than you did that day. It feels a lot more personal than that. It feels like *you lost because you're not as good as those other people*. They're more intelligent, better people, who will go on to do things greater than what you can do. They're just more worthwhile.

Of course, this idea is ridiculous! A pageant is judged by flawed human beings who have to make a snap judgment about dozens of people after seeing them for a very short period of time. Their subjective opinions are expressed in a numeric score for four specific categories of competition. The highest score wins. When you think about it, that's kind of a crazy process!

Obviously, it has nothing to do with which person is "better" or "more valuable." Each of us is equally precious, from Miss America to those who have never had the opportunity to compete. But this is hard to remember, and even harder to believe, when you're sitting backstage watching ten other young women who have been judged more worthy than you advance to the next round of competition.

"Why did You let this happen to me, when I've prayed to You so much?" I shouted in my heart to God. "I thought this is what You wanted me to do. I was only doing what I thought You wanted me to do!"

And then I heard an insidious whisper inside me, "I must have been mistaken in thinking this is what God wants me to do." That doubt added to the negative thinking that was drowning out my life.

May God forgive me for my selfishness and lack of understanding. I felt that He had betrayed me.

I never imagined that this would be one of the best experiences of my life.

'I'm Never Doing This Again'

I had said it four years before, after I competed at the Miss Wisconsin Pageant. But this time, I really meant it. At least, I thought I did.

"It would have been interesting to see how she would have done with a better platform," some people said. Others said,

"She won talent, so it was obviously her interview that did her in. But how could she have expected to do well with that platform?" And still others advised, "If you come back, you might want to consider a more realistic platform."

More realistic? Abstinence *is* realistic. The majority of fifteen- to nineteen-year-olds today (fifty-three percent) are virgins. And that doesn't include "secondary virgins." What's not real about that?

Part of me wanted to walk away. If these pageant people couldn't handle this message, then maybe I should take it somewhere else. But if that's the case, isn't this the very group that needs to hear it the most? More to the point, was it the *message* that was the problem — or the *messenger*?

Facing the Truth

It was time for me to stop blaming others for losing and to take a good look at myself. I knew that I could have done better. I hadn't put my best foot forward in the competition. My negative thinking and lack of preparation had seriously held me back.

I certainly hadn't followed through on my "manifesto." I hadn't "seized the pen to write my own destiny." I was psyched out and intimidated by a very minor event in the grand scheme of my life — a state pageant competition. I was allowing small things, like my embarrassment about saying the word "sex," to get in the way of this incredibly major mission to reach teens about chastity!

God used my defeat to "shake me up"! We all need to be shaken up from time to time, to see what's really important, and to keep us from becoming lukewarm. I couldn't settle for a lukewarm approach to chastity. I had to go after my dream and get rid of the baggage inside me that was holding me back. I decided to return to Miss Pennsylvania the next year for another shot at the crown.

Mental Toughness, Spiritual Strength

One month before the Miss Pennsylvania Pageant, all the contestants got together for a weekend meeting to get to know one another and learn about the pageant competition week. This is typical among state pageants and is sometimes called "Prep Day."

The Miss Pennsylvania State Board brought in a motivational speaker to talk to us about "mental toughness." Most of the girls smirked and whispered to each other, "What does this have to do with pageants?" I later learned that it has everything to do with pageants, and more importantly, it has everything to do with life.

The speaker described a person who is "mentally tough" as the type of person who performs superbly under pressure. He used examples of famous athletes, politicians, and business executives who are masters in tense or crucial situations. Then he described individuals who are "not mentally tough." These persons don't do their best in high-pressure situations, have difficulty putting experiences of failure behind them, and don't live up to their potential.

"That sounds like me!" I thought.

He went on to talk about ways to become "mentally tough" and recommended the book *Toughness Training for Life* by Jim Loehr. A few weeks after his extremely helpful presentation, I went out and bought this book.

Although it isn't very spiritual, the ideas and philosophies that this book expresses were just what I needed. Combining these ideas with my faith, I was able to extricate myself from the web of negative thinking and focus on my goals. By becoming "mentally tough," I became spiritually strong! Rather than looking inward at myself, I started to look outward at the world and discover ways that I could make it a happier, more beautiful place for others. I was more prepared to give of myself — and more prepared to stand with courage in the face of opposition.

Trial Number Two — Miss Pennsylvania the Second Time Around

I returned to Miss Pennsylvania with a fresh outlook, inspired to do my very best, and to do it for the Lord. It was one of the best weeks of my life! I made great friends and had a fantastic time, truly enjoying this experience to the fullest.

I felt very strong in every phase of competition and performed with a lot of mental toughness and spiritual strength. I felt ready to win.

But much to my disappointment, I didn't win. I was third runner-up, and my friend Mayra won. We had won our local titles at the same pageants for the past two years and were very close friends. We even called each other "pageant sisters." I was so happy for Mayra — but deeply disappointed for myself! I didn't understand. I believed that I was fully prepared to take on my mission. But, although I didn't see it at the time, this disappointment was really a blessing. God was giving me another valuable year to prepare myself for His work. It wasn't God's time for me to win. Although *I* didn't know it, He knew that I still wasn't ready for the mission that lay ahead.

> For everything there is a season, and a time for every matter under heaven.
>
> — ECCLESIASTES 3:1

When I went to the Miss America Pageant to cheer on Mayra, I was so proud of the wonderful young woman that she was. I understood that if God chose to bless me with the opportunity to compete at Miss America and to speak about chastity on a national level, He would give me the tools that I needed. But I needed to be open to His will. I needed to work not for my own glory, but for His.

Trial Number Three — A New Platform?

After my second attempt at Miss Pennsylvania, I asked the judges for advice on ways to improve, since I was eligible to compete one more year. They seemed to be extremely uncomfortable with my question. "We're not permitted to tell you anything," one of them said. But another said, "I know it's tough, but keep the platform, and keep plugging away at it."

I thought about those words over and over. "I know it's tough, but keep the platform. . . ." It *was* tough. My interviews weren't the "fluffy," lighthearted kind that I had seen on interview tapes. They were intense sessions of questioning on issues such as condom distribution in schools, abortion, sex education programs, homosexuality, high school day-care centers, and other hot-button issues. Most of the twelve minutes of my interview time was spent convincing skeptical judges that my platform was realistic.

And again, there was the never-ending gossip, the "ugly underbelly" of the pageant experience. "How could she have expected to win with that platform?" . . . "Thank goodness that abstinence girl didn't win. Who wants to hear about that?" One of my favorite comments was from an audience member who recognized me after the pageant, blurting out, "You're the one with that no-sex thing!"

Fortunately, these comments didn't bother me very much and helped me develop a sense of humor, which became very important in my work! But people started to notice these comments, including my brothers. They advised me to switch to something a little easier or more "politically correct."

"For competing in pageants, another platform would be better. Then after you win, you can talk about whatever you want," they said.

That idea seemed pretty valid. But, somehow, I didn't feel comfortable with changing my platform, especially after praying about it. No, if I was going to win, I was going to do it without watering down my convictions. I put it in God's hands.

Trial Number Four — Roadblocks in Pennsylvania

I thought about my vision of what I wanted my year to be like if I became Miss Pennsylvania or even Miss America. My dream was to have an extremely busy year, where every single day I was speaking to teens and young adults all over the country about chastity. I wanted to make it fun for the students so that they would be enthusiastic about this upbeat message, rather than thinking that chastity wasn't any fun. I wanted to make a difference by reaching millions of people!

But because I didn't have many ties to Pennsylvania, I had a hard time finding opportunities to speak to teens. I sent out a letter to local schools and churches and accompanied it with an outline of my presentations. But when I would make a follow-up call, I was generally told, "We don't have a problem with that here," or, "This is a religious message — that's not our area of concern," or even, "We don't like to have these types of political issues in our school."

Ultimately, I wasn't able to get into *any* Pittsburgh schools or churches to speak to students, probably because I didn't know anybody outside of Duquesne University and St. Mary of Mercy Church, where I was a cantor. The general attitude seemed to be, "Who is this girl who wants to come in and speak to our students about sex?"

I now tangibly realized the power of the crown. Having a title like Miss Pennsylvania would open so many doors! If I really wanted to reach people, I needed to win.

Wisconsin — Cold State, Warm Hearts

Fortunately, my message received a much warmer welcome in Wisconsin. My vacations were filled with speaking engagements in high schools and extensive work with the Milwaukee Best Friends girls. At first, it was nerve-wracking and very exhausting. Remember, I used to have a hard time just saying the words "sex" and "virgin"! Now, I had to use those words a number of times a day with large groups of teens. They were respectful and attentive, but I was *really* nervous!

As I spoke, there were moments when I sensed without a doubt that the Holy Spirit was flowing through me, giving me the courage, insight, and compassion I needed to touch people's hearts. When I was able to let go of my fear and let Him take over, amazing things happened! I left almost every presentation feeling that I had reached most of the students. This brought me so much joy and happiness!

I had one more year to compete in the Miss America program, before I exceeded the age limit of twenty-four. I was eligible to compete in Pennsylvania or Wisconsin, because I was a full-time student in one state and a permanent resident in the other. Although I had made many friends through the Miss Pennsylvania Pageant, my heart was in Wisconsin. This was where I had grown up, where I had attended college, where my parents lived, and where most of my friends were. This was also where I had done most of my work with teens. I decided to compete in the Miss West Allis Pageant, a preliminary to Miss Wisconsin, and won.

It was "no holds barred"! The more speaking I did, the more requests I had to speak, as news about my work spread among the schools. I got to know all of the Milwaukee Best Friends girls as a role model speaker and became familiar with the other abstinence programs around the state of Wisconsin. I created a partnership with the Wisconsin Department of Health and Family Services' abstinence efforts and traveled to Washington, D.C., several times to work with Best Friends on a national level.

In the midst of all of these things, I had finished my master's degree at Duquesne and was working on an artist diploma. I had spent two summers studying opera in Italy. I was teaching a class at Duquesne University in addition to my private voice studio, and I had many good friends.

My life was very full! But I was longing for something more . . .

Last Chance

The Miss Wisconsin competition week was right around the corner, and with it was my last chance to compete in the Miss America program. Doug, my mentor, liked to say, "It's do or die." For some reason, that always made me really nervous!

Mom and I had prayed novenas to St. Thérèse in the past for major events in my life. This time, my whole family and many close friends also prayed the novena with us, that if it was God's will, I would win the Miss Wisconsin title. I had been very close to St. Thérèse for a long time. With a "major league prayer team" behind me, I knew that she would pull out all the stops in interceding for me.

"In a week, it will be all over," I thought as I climbed into the car to drive up to Oshkosh for the pageant. "My life may never be the same."

That was exactly what I was hoping for.

Trial Number Five — Singing Disaster

That week at the Miss Wisconsin Pageant, I felt stronger than ever before in every phase of competition. My interview went great, I was in good shape for swimsuit, and I had enjoyed answering my onstage questions. The only hurdle left in the preliminary competition was my strongest area, talent.

After my Friday afternoon talent rehearsal, I received a note from Doug, who was among the local directors watching in the audience. "Can you hear the accompaniment tape up there? You're way out of tune on those high notes!"

I was surprised — I never sang out of tune. What did he mean by this? He must be mistaken.

Then I recalled that sometimes when I was practicing this piece, I had a tendency to go sharp in the upper range. For my second run-through, I asked the sound technicians to increase the accompaniment tape volume in the monitors so that I could hear it more clearly. I thought it went great.

When I saw Doug, I said, "I really nailed it!"

Doug almost had a fit. "Nailed it? You sounded awful! You were incredibly sharp on the high notes — you weren't even close to the right pitch!"

I was shocked. Could this be true? The tape's orchestration was dense but not very penetrating, so when I sang in my upper range, it was difficult to hear the accompaniment. I couldn't believe it. Why was this happening now? Suddenly, I was absolutely terrified to sing.

Singing that night was one of the most stressful experiences of my life! I was completely out of tune. The judges' disappointed expressions said it all. I couldn't understand it — my strongest area of competition had become my undoing!

In addition, the young woman who won the talent competition the previous night won swimsuit that evening. (After each night of preliminary competition, awards were given to the contestants with the highest scores in swimsuit and talent.) Catherine now had two preliminary awards — and I had none.

That night on the bus, as twenty-four weary contestants were being brought back to the hotel, I heard some whispering, "It's over now. Why should we even keep trying?" "She's won it already." "The judges have obviously picked her."

In my heart, I knew that it wasn't over. The interview and onstage questions were always the most important, and I had done well in these areas. This was the moment of truth, my *real* "trial by fire." Did I have the determination and mental toughness to stay positive, to stay focused when things looked hopeless? I had come too far to succumb to discouragement now. I had a choice: to stand with courage or watch my dream die.

Courage Under Fire

Even though I walk through the valley of the shadow of death,
   I fear no evil;
   for thou art with me;

thy rod and thy staff,
they comfort me.

— PSALM 23:4

I awoke Saturday morning in hopeful prayer, asking God to prevent me from becoming discouraged and instead to clothe me in faith, love, charity, and especially — fortitude! During our afternoon break, I walked along the lake by our hotel, listened to music, and prayed. (The *Star Wars* soundtrack was my favorite, and it really kept me pumped up!) "Without God, I can do nothing. But with God, I can do all things," I repeated to myself over and over. All day, I focused on this meditation, as I watched the waves splashing into the shoreline and dancing in the sunlight.

The Holy Spirit was always with me in a special way during my performances, ever since the opening night of *My Fair Lady* during my freshman year of high school. I knew that He would be with me again that night. If only I could trust in Him completely! This was the challenge: In the face of discouragement, to have faith, to trust, and to believe. I begged St. Thérèse, my spiritual sister, to intercede for me with Mary, my Mother and namesaint, and grant this request — if it was God's will.

And I asked for resignation to that will, whatever it was, because God tells us:

My thoughts are not your thoughts,
neither are your ways my ways.

— ISAIAH 55:8

There was a good chance that I wouldn't win. This dream that I had worked toward for years could be gone forever. Even if that happened, I wanted to remember that God has a plan that is far beyond my understanding, and He is always in charge!

I thought about how far I had come over the past few years and how wonderful the Miss America program had been in bringing about so much growth in my life. Certainly, the scholarship money would be great in paying off my hefty student loans. But beyond this material benefit, I had gained things no one can put a price on — close friends, my experiences speaking to teens, courage, compassion, a deeper spiritual life, wonderful memories. Regardless of this pageant's outcome, these things would be with me forever. As Doug reminded me over and over again, I was going into tonight's competition with nothing to lose.

Competition Finals

The Saturday night competition flew by in a blur. Hearing my name announced in the Top Ten was both exciting and a relief. Then the swimsuit competition — definitely the most mindless part, when all you have to do is walk (without tripping, if possible). Talent — it didn't go well, but I put it out of my mind. Evening wear — no onstage question tonight, just modeling the gown. (On the final night, only the Top Five are interviewed onstage.)

And then, time suddenly seemed to stand still. I was standing among the Top Ten behind the gold curtain, awaiting the Top Five cut at the end of the emcee's song. My heart was pounding, my throat was tight, and my knees felt like they were going to give out from shaking! I had been at this part of a state pageant before, but this time was different. It was my last chance.

Three names were called for the Top Five, and then mine! I exuberantly sat down on one of the stools among the other four finalists. The emcee and Kellye Cash, Miss America 1987, asked each of us two different questions — one from our résumé, and one on our platforms — which she read from cards. To be on this stage, to have this chance, to share my convictions and my heart with the audience — this is what I looked forward to most of all! As I answered my questions, I had a tremendous sense of peacefulness and joy! I was completely in the moment, and I wanted it to last forever.

But after my onstage interview was over, time couldn't go by fast enough! I was anxious and exhausted. My talent performance had been poor. Could this be the end of my long journey? Would this be the death knell of my dream?

I had no idea what was going to happen. It was in God's hands.

Moment of Truth

All twenty-four of us contestants were now onstage for the crowning of the new Miss Wisconsin. Everything was happening in slow motion. The second runner-up had been named — only two of us were left! Catherine and I looked at each other. On some level, I think that each of us had known it was going to be like this. We had shared a tough, healthy competition. Both of us gave it our all and had come to respect each other. We had become friends.

We hugged and held hands. For no one who has ever experienced it, it may be hard to understand, but that moment is a real bonding experience. Even though you want to win yourself, you also really care about the other contestant. She is the only one in the whole world who is experiencing the same moment and the same feeling that you are — a moment and a feeling that have never been, and never will be again!

"First runner-up is Miss Racine, Catherine Apilado! *The new Miss Wisconsin is Mary-Louise Kurey!*"

At that moment, the shock of joy that shot through me was unbelievable! I felt like I had been zapped with a lightning bolt! (A very happy lightning bolt!) I had no idea what I was doing, how I was reacting, or what was happening around me! But every inch of my soul was crying out, "God, thank You!" I was overcome by an awesome, indescribable feeling!

My family and friends in the audience were ecstatic. I could see them jumping up and down in the aisles, cheering, clapping, and hugging each other. I could hear my sister yelling, "All right,

Mary-Louise!" My brothers were shouting, "Way to go, Bunny!" Even Nana was jumping around (and she was eighty-seven years old at the time!), trying to take pictures in the midst of the chaos! Dad was crying, as usual, and Mom had a big smile on her face, looking exhausted from the evening's drama.

As Jill Patzner, the previous Miss Wisconsin, placed the precious Miss Wisconsin crown on my head, I felt like my heart was going to physically burst, because I couldn't handle the joy of it all! A blur of memories flooded my mind: the discouragements and setbacks of the week that led up to this moment . . . the times long before when I had lost hope . . . the people who supported me and challenged me to go after my dreams . . . the wonderful experiences speaking to teens . . .

My journey hadn't been a pretty one. But tonight, at the final hour, my dream became a reality.

I took the runway with a song in my heart, realizing that God doesn't possess just a couple of gifts, but *infinite* gifts!

My friend, God wants to give you *all that you desire in your life, and more!* Be open to Him! Take the risk of letting Him be in charge! It can be hard — sometimes you have to "cast out into deeper waters." Sometimes you have to go through a "trial by fire." Sometimes you have to believe in Him and in yourself even in the midst of discouragement and defeat.

But when you open your heart, "put out into the deep," and persevere, you'll discover an abundance greater than anything you could ever imagine. God's mission for you is so special! His plan for you is so awesome! If you let Him, He'll rock your world!

A fuller, more exciting life awaits you! Are you ready to say "yes"?

> Thy steadfast love, O LORD, extends to the heavens,
>   thy faithfulness to the clouds.
> Thy righteousness is like the mountains of God,

thy judgments are like the great deep;

man and beast thou savest, O LORD.

How precious is thy steadfast love, O God!

The children of men take refuge in the shadow of thy wings.

They feast on the abundance of thy house,

and thou givest them drink from the river of thy delights.

For with thee is the fountain of life;

in thy light do we see light.

— PSALM 36:5-9

9

Stepping Into a Larger World

Finally, be strong in the Lord and in the strength of his might. Put on the whole armor of God, that you may be able to stand against the wiles of the devil. For we are not contending against flesh and blood, but against the principalities, against the powers, against the world rulers of this present darkness, against the spiritual hosts of wickedness in the heavenly places. Therefore take the whole armor of God, that you may be able to withstand in the evil day, and having done all, to stand. Stand therefore, having girded your loins with truth, and having put on the breastplate of righteousness, and having shod your feet with the equipment of the gospel of peace; above all taking the shield of faith, with which you can quench all the flaming darts of the evil one. And take the helmet of salvation, and the sword of the Spirit, which is the word of God.

— EPHESIANS 6:10-17

I had no idea what to expect next. The two months between Miss Wisconsin and Miss America were filled with chaos, paperwork, and excitement! Those in the news media were fascinated by my "controversial" platform, and they kept me busy with interviews for articles, news programs, and talk shows. Some of the headlines reached across the globe, from a newspaper in Ireland to online newsmagazines in Argentina and Nicaragua. (My favorite caption was "Mary-Louise Kurey: Un-sex symbol" underneath my picture in the *New York Times — London Edition*.) There were also endless wardrobe fittings for my Miss America gowns, which were generously donated by dressmakers in Wisconsin.

But the best part of these two months were the many amazing opportunities God gave me to speak about chastity at conferences and events across the United States. One week, I found myself on Capitol Hill, addressing members of Congress at the National Parents' Day Reception and at conferences at the *Washington Times*. The next week, I was in San Antonio, Texas, speaking to leaders in education and public health at the National Leadership Summit on Abstinence.

I could hardly believe how God had transformed my life! Just one year before, I was struggling to overcome negative thinking as I pursued my graduate studies in Pittsburgh, not really sure of where I was going. Now, I was traveling across the country as a national spokesperson on chastity and abstinence! God is so good to me — I'm not worthy of all of these blessings!

The highlight of my summer was meeting Elayne Bennett, the founder and president of the Best Friends Foundation. This is the character-building program I had been working with for a few years, which inspires thousands of girls across the United States to reject sex, drugs, and alcohol, so they can rise above adversity in their lives and achieve their dreams. Elayne is a great example of how one person can touch the lives of hundreds of thousands of others. Her dynamic vision, courage, and determination to make a difference are a tremendous inspiration to me. I was so honored and humbled when she designated me to be a national spokesperson for her organization! Elayne is my hero, my complete woman — she is a great mother, a great wife, and a great career woman who has truly made a difference in the futures of teens across the country.

A Battle Inside Me

But preparing for Miss America wasn't all inspiration and opportunity. In fact, it was more like going into spiritual warfare! A battle was waging inside of me. There were moments when the thought of competing at the Miss America Pageant was incredibly terrifying! I couldn't put the nightmare of my singing performance during the Miss Wisconsin competition out of my mind; especially because it was hashed over and re-hashed by many people, most of whom I had never even met.

One friend called me while browsing a pageant website, thinking that I'd be interested in the spin. "Somebody wrote here, 'No one needs to worry about Wisconsin. I just saw her tape and she shouldn't have even won.' Uh-oh, here's another that says, 'How could Wisconsin have a master's in singing and be so bad?' Here's one about you, too. 'Wisconsin is a good speaker, but between her platform and lack of talent, she'll be a nonfactor.' "

Another friend called who was unable to attend the Miss Wisconsin Pageant. "I just watched the tape. You told me it was bad, but I didn't realize it was *that* bad. I didn't even know you *could* be that bad. What happened?" Talk about humbling! So much for pageants being an "ego trip"!

I couldn't escape criticism even in Oshkosh, the city where the Miss Wisconsin Organization is located. During a practice interview for Miss America, one of my "judges" said, "People make the excuse that you didn't sing well at Miss Wisconsin because you were nervous. But if you can't handle your nerves at a state pageant, how will you be able to handle it when you're competing at Miss America, where the stakes are fifty times higher?"

This was the question that weighed on me heavily. I didn't have an answer.

The Silver Lining

But God used my disappointing talent performance to re-veal to me something very beautiful — something that to this day affects the way I look at myself.

I had always identified myself as a singer, and over the years I had come to value myself based on my level of singing. In other words, my self-worth depended on how well I sang. But when I won Miss Wisconsin, my singing performance was poor. I didn't win based on my singing; I won because of the person that I was. The judges were impressed with my interview, my public speaking skills, the passion that I had for my platform, my personality, and the work that I had done with teens.

Although it hurt to hear people's uncomplimentary comments about my talent performance, on a deeper level, I learned that *my worth lies in something far more meaningful than having a pretty voice. My worth — as well as yours — lies in being children of God!* This is truly our identity!

Remember in Chapter 4 when we talked about my friend Susan's story? She compromised almost everything in high school for popularity. She, like many of us, found her value and worth in what other people thought of her. She felt that she had to be something that she wasn't for people to like her. She did things to impress people. But when she achieved her goal of great popularity, she wasn't happy.

My friend, it doesn't matter if you're the captain of the football team, the smartest kid in the class, the school "rebel," or a quiet kid that doesn't say much. Those things have no impact on your "love-ability"! *You are lovable and special not because of those superficial reasons but because of the person that you are!*

Once we're able to accept that, we're free to love others more! When we acknowledge that we are lovable — and loved — because of who we are, we stop looking at ourselves critically and instead look out at the world. We think, "What can I do to make this a better place for others?"

Keeping this lesson close to my heart helped me to approach Miss America with the right attitude about my singing. I no longer felt that I had something to prove. I just felt grateful for the talents that God had given me and wanted to use them for His glory.

Another Side of Sacrifice

Shortly before I left for the Miss America Pageant, my sister, a captain in the U.S. Air Force, called from her base in Omaha. She said to my parents, "When I came into the office today, the guys showed me an editorial column in the paper that mentions Mary-Louise. It's not too good!"

Dad found the article online. It was written by nationally syndicated columnist Ellen Goodman, whose articles appear in hundreds or perhaps thousands of newspapers across the country. This article said a lot of uncomplimentary things about a variety of famous people. Underneath a paragraph ripping on Howard Stern, she wrote:

"Contestant Mary-Louise Kurey, Miss Wisconsin, strutted her stuff while running on an abstinence platform. For this stunning delivery of a mixed message, we send her a virtual sex object."

Her criticism had the opposite effect of what was intended. I was totally pumped up about it! I thought, "I must really be making waves, if this woman whom I've never met is attacking me in a national column!" I also was relieved that her argument was so weak. A virgin can't wear a swimsuit? Talk about being out of touch!

"Yeah! No one kicks a dead dog!" I cheered to my parents, who were reading the computer screen in dismay. "I must really be making an impact!"

"Yes, you are! And your year is just beginning!" said Mom, giving me a hug.

Dad had tears in his eyes. "You're right, Mary-Louise," he said, trying to get out a choked laugh. "Thatta girl! That's the way to look at it."

I had seen my father weep many times before — during graduations, weddings, and other sentimental occasions. In fact, it was a joke in our family that Dad usually got a little teary-eyed at important events. But I don't ever remember seeing him cry from sadness. He was hurt by what was written about me.

For the first time, I understood that my work didn't only involve my own personal sacrifice — it was hard on my family, too. But through it all, they stood by me faithfully, with lots of love and plenty of courage.

A Telling Decision

Another challenge came my way that summer before the Miss America Pageant: the pageant community's opposition to my platform. As I mentioned earlier, before I won Miss Wisconsin, there was a lot of pressure to change my platform. After I won Miss Wisconsin, I assumed that this problem would go away, because I had proven that a person could win a competitive state pageant with this issue. Instead, just the opposite happened! The pressure to change my platform became more intense. Even the Miss Wisconsin Organization's state board was encouraged to switch my platform to something a little more "politically correct." During one of my wild 'n' crazy prep sessions with Sue and Lou Captain, Miss Wisconsin Organization directors who prepared me for Miss America, we discussed this issue.

Sue suggested, "If you want, you could change to something like character education, which already is a part of your platform, and just have abstinence be a part of that. That might go over better." She paused. "The decision is up to you. Whatever you decide, we'll support you a hundred percent."

I thought for a moment. "No, I don't want to change. Character development is an important part of choosing abstinence, but this message is too important to water down."

"That's fine with us," Sue said. "And I think that when they see what you've already done with this and what you could do with it as Miss America, they'll change their minds. I just don't think that they've realized it can be this good."

Who could ask for more supportive friends? Another state board might have forced me to change to a different platform.

But Sue and Lou believed. Their wisdom, practicality, humor, and confidence in me helped me to "stand with courage" as I embarked on yet another exciting adventure — competing at the Miss America Pageant.

10

Behind the Scenes at Miss America

Are not two sparrows sold for a penny? And not one of them will fall to the ground without your Father's will. But even the hairs of your head are all numbered. Fear not, therefore; you are of more value than many sparrows.

— MATTHEW 10:29-31

Most people know the Miss America Pageant only as a Saturday night TV show that happens every September. But for contestants, it's a two-and-a-half-week endurance contest that starts with four days at Disney World in Orlando, followed by two weeks in Atlantic City. The competition stretches over the last seven days, culminating in the Saturday night finals, which is televised live and watched by millions. Competing at this pageant is indescribable — no one knows what to expect until you actually get there. Every day is an adventure, with triumphs, setbacks, and unexpected snafus! Expect the unexpected!

Phase One: Orlando

My journey began at a small airport in Appleton, Wisconsin. An enthusiastic band of supporters was there to send me off — my family, friends, Miss Wisconsin volunteers, television news cameras, and Sue, who held a sign that said, "May the Force be with you." When I arrived at the airport in Orlando with my traveling companion, Ruth, it was easy for us to recognize the other contestants. They were all very outgoing — and they all had a ton of luggage! Disney was incredibly hot, but it was fun getting to know the girls as we toured the parks, did video production segments, and attended receptions, dinners, and lots of meetings.

Mass — Disney-Style

I wanted to attend Mass that Sunday morning, but I was scheduled to be in a video shoot with the rock group "98 Degrees."When I spoke to the coordinators from the Miss America Organization (MAO), they immediately rescheduled me to accommodate my wish, and even took me to Mass!

The Mass was at the outdoor terrace of the Polynesian Resort.When we arrived, the ladies from the MAO introduced me to the priest, telling him that I was Miss Wisconsin and that I was the only Miss America contestant who had asked to attend Mass that Sunday. (This wasn't really a big deal, though — most of the contestants weren't Catholic, and they probably didn't feel comfortable asking to attend church.)

When the priest was making announcements at the end of Mass, he introduced me and said that they would be praying for me! The congregation's enthusiastic applause reminded me that although I was "in the trenches" of Miss America activities, the chance to compete at Miss America was a very special opportunity given to me by God.

In Orlando, I made some good friends among the other contestants. Miss Michigan and I toured the parks together and watched the Main Street Electrical Parade from the riverboat in the Magic Kingdom. I must admit that Audrey and I were so engrossed in our interesting conversation with several of the other contestants that we hardly watched the parade!

Our final night at Disney was the Miss America Boardwalk Bicycle Parade.A large crowd gathered to watch the Miss America contestants ride down the Disney Boardwalk on two-person bicycles, wearing our state T-shirts. Sue designed mine: a black T-shirt with "Wisconsin" written in a Holstein cow pattern, and a cow-print sequined baseball cap and hip bag. Definitely a crowd favorite! What a great way to end our time in Orlando! It seemed like every day was better than the last.

Phase Two: Atlantic City

On Labor Day, we all boarded a charter flight into Atlantic City. With fifty-one contestants and two-and-a-half weeks of competition, everyone had something go wrong at least once! My nemesis was the suit I was going to wear for the arrival press conference. First, it got damaged in the suitcase on my flight to Orlando, when something spilled onto my black shoes and got black shoe dye all over the yellow jacket. Then it got covered with blue lint from the blanket I huddled under on the flight to Atlantic City. I didn't know whether to laugh or cry when I took off the blanket and saw my yellow suit covered with blue fuzz, moments before stepping off the plane to meet the national media! What a first impression! Fortunately, the reporters were flocking to other contestants when we arrived and were not very interested in Miss "Badger State"!

As one might expect, our schedule in Atlantic City was not as laid back as it had been at Disney World. The days were long and tiring. We were usually picked up from our hotels around seven in the morning and returned around eight at night. There were also some events in the evenings, like a hospital benefit or a dinner with sponsors. In our "spare time," we had many other things to take care of, such as visiting supporters, keeping up with current events for the interview, and alleviating stress by working out!

On the second day of rehearsals, the choreographer said, "Now we're going to learn the production number for Saturday night. This will be performed only by those of you who don't make the Top Ten." I felt this horrible sinking feeling inside. "Will that be me?" a small voice asked from within. As I looked around at the other contestants, I could tell they were thinking the same thing.

During rehearsals, I became good friends with Lucy (Miss West Virginia) and Elaine (Miss Wyoming). Elaine's platform was also abstinence, and she worked with the chastity movement called "True Love Waits." They are both very special young women with a strong faith. We would hang out and sometimes even pray together during rehearsal "dead time," when we were sitting around waiting.

Rehearsals consumed most of each day. There were always several photographers taking candid pictures of us — you never knew what picture of you might end up in the paper! During the second week in Atlantic City, our rehearsals onstage typically had a large audience of state and local pageant volunteers. We were a very popular group!

The only place of refuge from onlookers was Sleepy Hollow, a room with about thirty cots where one could grab a few winks of sleep on breaks. Unfortunately, these breaks were few and far between; most days, we were given only one break — our lunch hour.

My Daily Retreat

I loved lunchtime! Each morning, I signed up for a practice room to rehearse my talent during lunch, usually taking the last time slot so that I could have a room for almost a half hour. When lunch was called, I would head down to the galley with the first group. After eating, I'd handle any media interviews that had been scheduled, then move on to my favorite part of the day: practicing my talent! It's ironic, but my singing had gone from a source of stress at Miss Wisconsin to a source of joy and peace at Miss America.

During those short but wonderful practice sessions, it was just Jesus, my singing, and me. These were like a small retreat for me each day. I'd start with about five minutes of prayer, then warm up with some vocal exercises, then do a couple of run-throughs of my talent song, the Italian aria "Il Bacio," meaning "The Kiss." Although my song was secular, I sang to glorify God, something that I strive to do with my singing every day. I don't always succeed, but in the environment of Miss America, I felt that my song was always a prayer to Him. Creating music this way brings me the greatest joy!

Miss America Goes Divorcée?

Toward the end of our first week in Atlantic City, Robert Beck, the CEO of the Miss America Organization, held a press conference to formally announce that the MAO was considering changing its eligibility requirements in order to allow young women who are divorced or have had abortions to compete. This news was very saddening, but it wasn't a surprise to the contestants. Over the summer, we were informed of these possible changes, and of course, many of us were not very enthusiastic.

Suddenly, I was a very sought-after interview from the media, probably because of my platform. Perhaps they saw that this change in the rules was the opposite of what I stood for through my work on chastity. They were right.

The next day, as I was doing a television interview for CNN, they asked my opinion about the change in the eligibility requirements. I had been asked not to comment on the subject, but I replied, "I understand why the Miss America Organization is considering this change, because of the widespread problems of divorce and abortion that are plaguing our society today. This is why abstinence education is so important and why I'm so dedicated to it."

That night, I heard from family and friends that they had seen my interview on CNN. "What a great plug for your issue!" they said. "You really turned that one around on them!" But although I received some good press for abstinence, I was concerned that I hadn't been outspoken enough in my disapproval of the rules change. (Two days after the Miss America finals, Robert Beck was fired from his position as CEO of the Miss America Organization. He is now suing the MAO to change its eligibility requirements, contending that they discriminate against divorced women and those who have had abortions.)

Spiritual Warfare

In the meantime, the media's reaction to my platform was beginning to weigh on me heavily. From CNN to E! (Entertainment News), my convictions were eliciting thinly veiled chuckles and condescending or even confrontational questions.

"Oh, so since you're a virgin, you think that everyone else should be forced to be also?"

"Come on! You really think that most teens are going to be abstinent?"

"What you propose isn't even natural. Expressing your sexuality is a healthy and natural thing to do. Don't you think that teens should just use protection?"

I was surprised at how entrenched the so-called "safe" sex message is in the media. I responded to their questions as pleasantly and competently as I could, but I had the feeling that some of the reporters were biased and would not fully or accurately present my point of view.

At first, this just rolled off my back. But as time went on, the doubt and skepticism began to take root. I remembered the advice that I had received, to switch to a different platform. "Maybe I should have done that," I thought. I wondered if I had been foolish to take on such a difficult issue in this unfriendly arena.

One night, as I was reflecting on an especially tough day, I realized that if I became Miss America, this kind of skepticism and mockery would increase a hundredfold. With that thought, I suddenly felt extremely hot and weak, and a wave of negative memories flooded my mind — school administrators who opposed my work, people who intentionally blocked my efforts, hurtful comments about my virginity, times that I hadn't spoken as well as I wanted to . . .

I cried to myself, "It's too much! I'm not strong enough to do this! I'm in way over my head." I wondered if my efforts had really even made a difference or if I was just wasting my time. Was it arrogant of me to believe that I could take on such a countercultural issue — and hope to make a positive impact on people's lives?

Depressed and discouraged, I called Lois, a spiritual director and close friend of my parents. She had given me some wonderful guidance before I left for Miss America, "to prepare you for spiritual combat," as she put it. She and her prayer group were praying for me, and she told me to call her whenever I needed to.

Lois didn't seem to be surprised by what I had to say. "This is the spiritual warfare that I had told you I thought would happen. The Lord is using you in a powerful way, Mary-Louise, and so the devil is now on the attack. These negative thoughts you're having are from the devil. Don't give in to them. When you feel this despair, call on the name of Jesus. His name is very powerful, and He will dispel these fears and fill you with the strength and wisdom that you need to do His work."

I found comfort in her words. After hanging up the phone, I followed her advice. My whole being silently called on the name of Jesus. Slowly, peacefulness and consolation began to seep into my troubled heart. I picked up my Bible. Over the past couple of years, I had become more comfortable with private, prayerful reading of God's Word, and had discovered a love for Scripture. It was always a great source of inspiration and guidance during difficult times.

What happened that night I will remember for the rest of my life. As I skipped to parts from my favorite books — the Gospels, Ruth, Songs of Songs, and so on — my eyes rested on Isaiah, Chapter 62. As I read it, my heart burned within me. I couldn't believe my eyes! This passage was written thousands of years ago — but it sounded like it was written just for me.

> For Zion's sake I will not keep silent,
>   and for Jerusalem's sake I will not rest,
> until her vindication goes forth as brightness,
>   and her salvation as a burning torch.

The nations shall see your vindication,
    and all the kings your glory;
and you shall be called by a new name
    which the mouth of the LORD will give.
You shall be a crown of beauty in the hand of the LORD,
    and a royal diadem in the hand of your God.
You shall no more be termed Forsaken,
    and your land shall no more be termed Desolate;
but you shall be called My delight is in her,
    and your land Married;
for the LORD delights in you,
    and your land shall be married.
For as a young man marries a virgin,
    so shall your sons [Builders] marry you,
and as the bridegroom rejoices over the bride,
    so shall your God rejoice over you.

— ISAIAH 62:1-5

Every line, every word, spoke to me! *"For Zion's sake I will not keep silent . . ."* People had tried to keep me silent by encouraging me to change my platform. They had tried to stop my mission! But I had refused to compromise my beliefs because I felt that people needed to hear the truth, which will rise someday *"as a burning torch"*!

"The nations shall see your vindication . . ." Nations had already seen this "vindication," this truth, in the many articles about my work published in newspapers all over the country, and in other countries as well! These amazing blessings were truly the work of the Lord!

"And you shall be called by a new name which the mouth of the Lord will give . . ." I thought, "The new name God has given me is Miss Wisconsin! This was truly a gift from Him!"

"You shall no more be termed Forsaken, and your land shall no more be termed Desolate . . ." I thought, "Right now, some of those

reporters and pageant fans are looking at my platform and thinking that I am pretty pathetic, pretty "Forsaken." I certainly feel "Desolate." But no matter how I feel or what others think about me, God sees me as being His "Delight!" My work to promote chastity is truly blessed and "Married" to the Lord! And to use this analogy — *"As a young man marries a virgin. . ."* How thoughtful of God, to speak so obviously about chastity! This was great confirmation of my work.

But the part that moved me to tears of joy — and still does — is *"and as the bridegroom rejoices over the bride, so shall your God rejoice over you."* To think that God would *rejoice* about me! That He would rejoice in a little, flawed, wimpy person like me, who was discouraged at something as minor as a *pageant* . . . that God was looking down at my efforts and struggles, and rejoicing in my attempts!

This is what stays with me today — that God *rejoices* over our efforts to do His work. This is why, no matter how difficult things get or how discouraged we might become, we must always stand with courage! Whether or not we succeed in the world's eyes is relatively unimportant — we're doing the mission God wants us to do. He is rejoicing!

Phase Three: Competition Begins

That Sunday morning, competition week began. Rehearsal was scheduled starting early that morning, so it appeared that I wouldn't be able to attend Mass. I spoke with Georgia, my hostess in Atlantic City, and she was able to get permission for me to arrive at rehearsal a little late. She also arranged for me to be taken to Mass and suggested that I "ask around" to see if there were other contestants who wanted to come.

My friend Sylvia, Miss Connecticut, was also Catholic and was staying in the same hotel. Of all of the friendships that I made at Miss America, hers is the strongest — we keep in touch to this day! When I invited her to join me for Mass, she enthusiastically accepted, and we found a very early Mass at a small church near our hotel. After Mass, I told the priest that we were Miss America contestants, and I asked him for a special blessing. He was very kind and gave Sylvia and me a particularly beautiful blessing as we began our week of competition at the Miss America Pageant.

The next morning was my first phase of competition — the private interview. This is by far the most important aspect of competition. Beforehand, I was given a special opportunity — to receive Jesus in the Blessed Sacrament!

'Panis Angelicus'

One of the most precious memories of my whole life was that morning when my mother reverently brought the living presence of Jesus to me in Holy Communion. The MAO asked that she do this in a public place, to respect the rules regarding family members' contact with contestants. We stood by the elevator on my floor at the Taj Mahal hotel, with a beautiful view of the ocean and sky, and had a little prayer service. Then I received Jesus from the pyx that she carefully protected, and we prayed the special prayer to the Holy Spirit that we often say before important events. And as we prayed, we started crying! This was the realization of my dream! To be able to share this intimacy with Jesus as I was competing at Miss America is a beauty that is practically unsurpassed in life.

I was blessed to receive the Eucharist every day during that final week in Atlantic City. Jesus' living presence was true refreshment for my soul during this challenging time.

Interview

The day was stormy and cold. A hurricane was on its way! Sandbags lined the boardwalk outside the hotel. Standing by the window in the interview waiting area, I looked out at the gray, tumultuous waves crashing on the shore and listened to the tape "So Full of Deep Joy," recorded by the monks of Weston Priory.

"Lord, I am but a child, I do not know what I should say."
"Do not be afraid. I am with you . . ."

I knew that the interview would be difficult. I anticipated that most of the judges would probably have different values than I and remembered that the MAO had expressed serious reservations about my platform. But I also knew that the Holy Spirit would be with me throughout it all, to answer their questions with wisdom, knowledge, and understanding.

I worked very hard to prepare for this interview, doing extensive research on abstinence and related areas from a medical, sociological, and educational perspective. I had spoken about chastity at venues across the country, working with young people from a wide variety of socioeconomic and ethnic backgrounds. And I was the national spokesman for a highly respected program that provided abstinence-based character education to thousands of young women across the U.S. with outstanding results. I was ready.

As I walked into the room and gave my opening statement behind the Miss America podium, I realized that I was standing at the very podium where former Miss Americas Heather Whitestone and Nicole Johnson had stood — young women of faith and compassion who were role models to me and many others. What an extraordinary opportunity! I had nothing to lose!

The first half of my interview was the best interview of my life. The questions were very tough, but I handled them with knowledge, humor, and compassion. My content was good, and I felt a real connection with the judges.

Then for some reason, the tone of the interview suddenly changed. One of the judges (a former nun!) began to aggressively attack my views on abortion, abstinence, and even the scandals of President Clinton's administration. When I refused to back down from my convictions, several other judges joined her. I was determined not to compromise my beliefs — not after coming so far, with so much sacrifice! In what seemed like a few moments, there were five angry judges interrogating me! I was able to keep calm, using solid reasoning and facts to support my position. But I was disturbed by how confrontational my Miss America interview had become.

When I walked out, I felt as though I had been in front of a firing squad. Georgia gave me a big hug and asked, "How did it go?"

"I don't know," I said, baffled and concerned. "I've never had such a tough interview in my life. I've never even had anything close to that."

I called Doug, my coach, and told him everything that I could remember. "It sounds like you did a really good job," he said. "They were testing you, and you stood up to it. You didn't back down."

Was Doug right? Or had I blown it?

Talent

There wasn't much time to dwell on my interview, because I was doing the talent competition the next day. After the fiasco of my talent performance at Miss Wisconsin, I had left no stone unturned in my preparation, from the orchestration of my accompaniment tape to my movement onstage.

The only opportunity for contestants to rehearse their talent presentations on the Miss America stage is on the day that they are scheduled to compete in talent. My two run-throughs went well, except that I slipped on my train when I took a step back during the second rehearsal. "Solution: Don't take any steps backward tonight," I thought to myself. For some reason, this struck me as being really funny — probably because I'm always tripping!

Opening Night at Miss America

That night, the atmosphere was electric! The crowd was really pumped up! Backstage, all of us were running around hugging one another and saying, "I can't believe I'm here at Miss America! I can't believe it!" Minutes before the curtain went down (it was a huge sheet that was sucked into a hole in the middle of the stage), a group of us joined together in spontaneous prayer.

After the opening number, I headed to Sleepy Hollow to warm up. After all, no one would be sleeping during the pageant! I prayed to the Holy Spirit to be with me and to sing through me during my talent performance.

Then I turned to my spiritual sister. "St. Thérèse, you have been with me in a special way for so long. My family and friends have been praying this novena to you. Now is my moment of truth. Bring me a rose. If it is God's will, let me have a beautiful performance tonight. And let me sing not for my own glory, but for His."

Last-Minute Laugh

Minutes before my talent performance, I was standing in the wings of the stage when I suddenly felt like I wanted to do just one more vocal exercise to warm up. I knew this was ridiculous — I didn't need to warm up anymore, but I couldn't resist.

As I hurried farther into the wings, I let my long white train drag behind me, rather than picking it up like I usually did. A hostess called, "Where are you going?"

"I just want to do one more warm-up. I'll be right back."

"You don't have time!"

I looked back. She was right — the contestant right before me had already started. I had less than two minutes before my performance! Then I looked down. My white satin train was *black* — filthy from dirt on the stage! And here I was, about to step onto the competition stage of the Miss America Pageant for the first time with a dirty dress!

Fortunately, God gave me the presence of mind to laugh at myself at this tense moment! As I sat down to brush off the train as quickly as I could, several of the hostesses hurried over to help. They were surprised by my laughter, but I couldn't help it! Talk about getting what I deserved! It was my own "obsessive-ness" — wanting to do a last minute warm-up I didn't need — that had put me into this ridiculous situation!

And then it was time. The moment of truth was upon me, when I would discover the answer to that question that had haunted me ever since the Miss Wisconsin Pageant: "If you were nervous then, how will you handle the nerves when the stakes are fifty times higher?"

Before I walked onto the stage, I prayed, "St. Thérèse, give me a rose in a beautiful performance. Holy Spirit, I place every-thing in Your hands."

St. Thérèse's Rose

One of my favorite movies is *Chariots of Fire*. In the film, a devout Scottish missionary named Eric Liddell is a great runner. His sister, who is very close to him, is deeply troubled that her brother is taking time from his missionary work to train for the Olympics. She tells him that she is afraid of what this might do to his soul. She firmly believes that his running aspirations are a distraction from God.

One day, Eric pulls his sister aside and explains to her how his running actually glorifies and pleases God. He says, "God made me for a purpose. But He also made me *fast*! And when I run, I feel His pleasure."

I had always wondered what Eric meant by that — to feel God's pleasure. That must be an amazing experience! To do some-thing so completely in unity with God that you *feel His pleasure!*

That night onstage at Miss America, as I started to sing, I imagined my grandfather, who introduced me to opera at a very young age, looking down on me, watching me. I could almost feel his presence, and I imagined that he was sitting among the judges and taking in my performance.

And then, St. Thérèse graced me with a beautiful rose. I was suddenly overcome by a tremendous joy and peace, and I felt as though I was resting on Jesus' heart. My whole being sang — without tension or fear or tripping or running out of air or going out of tune or any of the other things that I worried about so often. No worry crossed my mind, because I was completely filled with wonder at the beauty of God's love. I was so completely at peace and my heart was so filled with joy that I was able to sing totally for Jesus, and to sing like I'd never sung before.

At that moment, I knew what Eric Liddell meant. *As I sang, I truly could feel God's pleasure!* It was as if the whole universe was in harmony, as if there was no hatred or jealousy or anger or violence or loneliness, but only love — God's unending, perfect love, filling all of our hearts and overcoming, overflowing the world. This is what Eric Liddell meant — to concretely experience the inexplicable, exquisite pleasure of God at my little song. This was the moment of a lifetime!

And then it was over, and I basked in the joy of that moment. In worldly terms, I didn't know if I had given "the performance of a lifetime." I didn't care. That wasn't important. Something far greater had happened.

God had given me true confirmation. In two minutes, He had dispelled the ghosts of past failures that plagued my heart and confirmed that my singing was a calling from Him, and that my singing brought Him pleasure. I knew then that I was born to sing. This was my epiphany. Whatever else happened at Miss America, nothing would be able to compare with this once-in-a-lifetime experience.

The Love of My 'Sisters'

When I returned to the dressing room after my performance, my fellow contestants crowded around me in an explosion of joy. They had been watching the talent performances on the monitors in the dressing rooms. Their happiness at my success was as sincere as if it had been their own.

As they showered me with hugs, compliments, and affection, I felt that this must be one of the happiest moments of my life. To have won the esteem and love of these accomplished, wonderful young women — my "sisters" in competition — was such an honor. It is the essence of the Miss America experience.

The Icing on the Cake

The time had come for the announcement of the preliminary awards in swimsuit and talent. The competition in my talent group was especially strong, and I stood among the other fifty contestants with a hopeful heart.

When my name was called as the talent winner, I was overwhelmed with joy! Heather French, Miss Kentucky, was the swimsuit winner. We took the famous Miss America runway together, and the crowd rose to its feet. I couldn't see my family (the auditorium was enormous and the flashing cameras were blinding), but I waved in their direction. I could see Sue and Lou standing up and cheering on the other side.

Suddenly, I heard a familiar voice nearby calling, "Mary-Louise!" I looked down, and Doug was running on the floor next to the runway, cheering and waving his arms! How he got through the security, I'll never know, but I was glad he was there!

Heather and I were brought to the winner's circle for media photos and interviews. And then, the real treat — seeing my family and friends at the post-pageant visitation for the first time since I had left Wisconsin two weeks before.

Everyone was so wonderful! Miss Hawaii and her supporters serenaded me as they put around my neck a beautiful lei of yellow and white flowers. The Wisconsin people were elated at this honor for our state. My friends from Pennsylvania came over to congratulate us, among them Mayra (the previous year's Miss Pennsylvania), Jamie, and Maria, who had competed with me. God had showered me with so many blessings! I couldn't believe it! I was a preliminary talent winner at Miss America!

That night in the hotel, I was too excited to sleep. I kept waking up and walking over to the table where my crystal trophy was, to make sure it really happened. The next day, Heather and I were bombarded with media interviews because of our preliminary wins. Of course, I didn't mind — I could take a break from practicing my talent for a day! By the time that night rolled around, though, I was totally wiped out! But it was time for the evening wear portion of the competition.

Evening Wear

The evening wear competition at Miss America involves just walking in your gown and answering one onstage question, which can be about almost anything in your life. The onstage question used to be the most nerve-wracking phase of competition for me. But Doug helped me realize that this was just like an ordinary conversation. He'd refer to the many lively discussions we had shared in his car, saying, "It's just like strapping in to the Volvo or sitting down for dinner with Loretta and Beth," friends he had introduced me to. This helped me to become more relaxed in this area of competition. My high level of comfort with onstage questions came in especially handy in this funny situation.

Former Miss America Shawntel Smith was asking the onstage questions, reading them from index cards. After I had stepped off the infamous Miss America "turntable" in my gown, I approached Shawntel, who greeted me warmly. Then she read, "You've been a nanny to a little boy for three-and-a-half years. What has this experience taught you?"

"Actually, Shawntel, I've never been a nanny!" I said with a smile. As I looked over her shoulder, I couldn't help but laugh as I observed, "I think you're on the wrong card. That's the card for the next contestant!"

Everyone had a big laugh about this little mix-up. The audience of several thousand onlookers seemed to enjoy this unusual Miss America moment, and even the crankiest judges chuckled at this unexpected situation. Shawntel put her arm around me and said to the audience, "This *is* a live show!" Then she paused before joking, "I guess the next girl knows what her question will be!"

She flipped back to my card and asked me how I have benefited from working with teens. What a wonderful question! This was something I loved to talk about, and my answer went well. (As I exited the stage, Shawntel was given another question for the next contestant.)

When I returned to the dressing room, the girls were wild with laughter, having observed the whole thing on the TV monitors. A number of them surrounded me, giving me hugs and exclaiming, "That was so hilarious!" "I'm glad that didn't happen to me!" "That was awesome how you handled that!" "You should have seen Shawntel's face!" "You are so funny, ML!"

Swimsuit

I had only one more phase to go in the preliminary competition — swimsuit. This is the toughest part before the pageant, but the easiest to do once you're there. Here's how it works: *Before* the pageant, you have to work out hard on a regular basis and avoid sweets and fatty foods, which I love! *During* the pageant, all you have to do is walk to the middle of the stage, stop, and walk off — it all takes only about fifteen seconds! Fortunately, I managed to do it without tripping or walking into the green sheets of fabric that swirled around each contestant as she entered the stage.

At the end of the show on Thursday night, we were all relieved to have completed the entire preliminary competition. Everyone had done interview, talent, evening wear, and swimsuit. Now, we were looking forward to the legendary Miss America Boardwalk Parade.

Phase Four: The Parade

On Friday night, the fifty-one of us were hauled over to a nifty little art gallery along the boardwalk to wait our turns in the parade. While there, I had the pleasure of talking with former Miss Americas Heather Whitestone and Kay Lani Raye Rafko. Since Elaine (Miss Wyoming) and I were at the end of the parade, we had about a two-hour wait. There was plenty of time to say the Rosary, read the Bible, and pray together.

When I finally entered the boardwalk, I was amazed at the thousands of cheering fans of all ages who lined the boardwalk for miles. It's a tradition for the people to call out "Show us your shoes!" so the contestants wear very distinctive shoes — some that are pretty, and some that are funny. My parade outfit was a black velvet "opera diva" type of dress with rhinestones and a hot pink wrap, but on my feet I had . . . *big, furry cow slippers!* Not glamorous, but warm, and the crowd had a good laugh.

The Wisconsin "herd" was seated together, dressed in their typical cow-print attire and waving signs that said, "May the Force be with you!" Doug ran along next to my car for a while, snapping photos and calling out bad jokes.

At the end of the parade, about forty friends and family members met in the lobby of my hotel and showered me with gifts and lots of love. This was so special! My sister even had a friend of hers there who was a priest. Everyone made a large circle around me and raised their hands over me as he gave me a special blessing. I realized that no matter what happened at Miss America the next night, this moment — surrounded by family and friends who had traveled hundreds of miles to support me — would always be one of my favorite memories.

Phase Five: The Finals

When I woke up the following morning, I realized that the next time I returned to the hotel, I would either be Miss America or never again have the chance to be Miss America.

Our day at the auditorium started early and seemed to drag on forever. No one was permitted to have any contact with us except for the production staff and auditorium hostesses. I think every single contestant cried at some point during rehearsals that day. We were all completely exhausted, and we also knew that it all would be over within ten hours . . . then six hours . . . then four hours. No one had any idea who had made the Top Ten, although many of the pageant "groupies" had been circulating lists of their picks. The stress was getting to everybody. Backstage, I saw Heather wiping away tears. I had a strange feeling as we sat together. We wished each other the best of luck.

Before the pageant, former Miss America Kellye Cash, who emceed the Miss Wisconsin Pageant, held a prayer session in the galley for any contestants who were interested. About thirty of us showed up. As we joined hands, I looked around at this amazing group of young women from all over the country and from a variety of faiths. I thought, "I will remember this moment forever."

Then we realized that in just an hour we'd be on national television, and all of us had red eyes, runny noses, and mascara running down our cheeks! We ended with a huge group hug, and then many little hugs, as contestants broke off in pairs to chat with each other and share final words of encouragement. Little did I know that this would be the last time I would have the opportunity to speak to many of these young women!

An hour later, we were live on national television in front of fifteen million people. The live audience was huge — at least twice the size of the preliminary nights' audiences. The cheering was deafening!

The parade of states flew by, and the hosts, Donny and Marie Osmond, were now announcing the Top Ten! For some reason, I felt very peaceful and calm during this nerve-wracking moment. Four names were called — and then I heard:

Miss Wisconsin, Mary-Louise Kurey!

My whole being erupted in joy! The calm and inner peace from moments before was left in the dust — I was incredibly excited! Then I heard Sylvia's name called for the Top Ten as well! I was so happy! My friend, who never put herself forward or sought prestige, was honored among the elite ten. And I remembered that passage from Scripture, "For those who honor me I will honor" (1 Samuel 2: 30).

(In a letter to me several months later, Sylvia wrote, "For both of us to make the Top Ten was really wonderful. That priest's blessing at Mass must have really worked!" She added, "I'm just kidding — I know that's not what a blessing is for.")

Other young women who made the Top Ten were Heather, Miss Kentucky, and Jade, Miss Illinois, with whom I had become close friends during the week as well.

Unfortunately, this was the first year that the Miss America Pageant had a new format. Rather than allowing the Top Ten to perform their talent on national television, only the Top Five would be permitted to compete in talent. This was hard for all of us. It made the stakes for getting into the Top Five that much higher.

There were few things that I've wanted in my life more than to perform my talent on national television. Swimsuit and evening wear were fun, but I had dedicated seven years of my life to my singing. To perform opera on national television — this would be an amazing experience, a dream come true.

The Top Five Cut

As I stood with the other nine finalists awaiting the next cut after swimsuit and evening wear, I felt the same strange peacefulness as before. I distinctly remember praying, "Lord, not my will but Your will be done. But God, if Your will is disappointing to me, help me to accept it with an open and joyful heart, without bitterness or regret."

The first name was called for the Top Five. Then the second. Then I started to feel nervous. Then the third! Then Jade's name was called! I was so happy for her! And then I realized — "Four people have been called, and Heather, Sylvia, and I are still in the Top Ten! Only one spot is left!" In that moment, the Holy Spirit filled me with courage and consolation, and I prayed, "Thy will be done." Then I heard:

Miss Kentucky, Heather French!

I was very sad to not make the Top Five. My quest, my pilgrimage, my dream to spread the message of chastity as Miss America was over. And not to be able to sing on national television — this was a great disappointment to me. I was close, but not close enough!

But as I stood with Sylvia and the others remaining behind the Top Five, I also felt very blessed. To be among the highest ten out of hundreds of thousands of young women who pursue this dream every year across the country — this was indeed something to be proud of!

I was grateful to have made the Top Ten . . . I was grateful for the opportunity to be among the fifty-one young women who were on that stage . . . I was grateful for my friendships with several of the contestants . . . I was grateful for the unwavering love of family and friends. And I was most grateful for the beautiful rose from St. Thérèse, an incredibly precious, life-changing experience that I would treasure forever.

As I look back on my performance at Miss America, I can honestly say that I have no regrets. After the pageant, many people said that if I had changed my platform, I would have been more successful. But I feel peaceful knowing that I never compromised who I am for the prestige of the crown. I also know in my heart that everything happens for a reason. Although sometimes we don't understand why things work out the way they do, we can take comfort in knowing that God is always in charge and that He has our best interests at heart.

As I sat next to Ruth, my beloved traveling companion, flying home from Atlantic City, I felt tears well up inside of me, and a lump grew in the back of my throat. I looked back on the amazing events of the past several months, the culmination of years of hard work and perseverance, sacrifice and hope. And now, what had it all come to? What was it all for? My dream of becoming Miss America would never be realized. It seemed that my opportunity to reach millions of people with the message of chastity was now gone forever. I thought that my journey had come to an end.

But God had other plans.

11

The New Sexual Revolution Takes Charge!

And he said to them, "The harvest is plentiful, but the laborers are few; pray therefore the Lord of the harvest to send out laborers into his harvest."

— Luke 10:2

The Miss America Pageant was just the beginning of my adventure. When I returned home to Wisconsin, I was amazed to find a full schedule of speaking engagements on chastity waiting for me, with bookings even six or eight months in advance! This exceeded my greatest hopes!

In addition, I never anticipated the wonderful enthusiasm of Wisconsin journalists for my performance at the Miss America Pageant and for my message. As I traveled across the state speaking at countless schools, churches, and community centers, reporters were there to "capture the moment." Video clips for the evening news . . . pictures with teens "in action" . . . live radio interviews before and after my presentations . . . my "quotables" in the next morning's paper — all of these things became part of my everyday life during that wonderful and fast-paced year. People seemed to be fascinated by "this outspoken, twenty-something virgin with a countercultural message." But it was God who made it all happen. He gave me the most amazing year of my life.

I was challenged in profound ways as I encountered completely new people each day all over the country. In the morning, I was a stranger; but by evening, I had been accepted as a friend — only to become a stranger again the next morning as I traveled to another unfamiliar place where I would touch the hearts of a new group of people, and they would touch mine.

These experiences gave me insight into rural and urban America that I had never imagined. The students I came into contact with made an unforgettable impact on my life. I was humbled by their sincere search for truth and real lasting love, especially when they entrusted to me their stories, their concerns, and their dreams. I was privileged to have the opportunity to touch their hearts and grateful that they touched mine as well.

I spoke to over two thousand teens a week about abstinence, and by the end of the year I had addressed over a hundred thousand teens and young adults! Through God's grace, my appearances and interviews on a variety of national and international television shows, radio programs, magazines, and newspapers touched the lives of over twenty-five million people.

On the Road With Miss Wisconsin

Although this may sound very glamorous, it was surprisingly grueling. In an average week, I did about fifteen presentations, while some weeks had over twenty! Schools and churches were the primary groups that were interested in my message, but I also spoke at a number of conferences, dinners, retreats, rallies, fund-raisers, camps, workshops, and even festivals. My days started early and ended late, typically beginning with an all-school assembly around 8:00 A.M. and ending around 9:00 P.M. or so with an evening presentation at a church, dinner, or nonprofit event. And then, there was the driving! Some days, I drove over three hundred miles! This is where my parents helped tremendously, especially my mother, who often drove while I returned phone calls, reviewed notes for my next talk, or caught a quick nap. I often went for three or four weeks straight without a day off, including weekends. I thought competing at Miss America was tiring, but the job of Miss Wisconsin was far more exhausting than I ever imagined!

Driving around in the official Miss Wisconsin car — a red 1999 Ford Escort with "Miss Wisconsin" on the doors and a license plate reading "Miss Wis" — I no longer had the anonymity that I had been used to. (No going out with dirty hair and no makeup!) But I didn't mind. It was a lot of fun to drive, and I got a kick out of seeing the crown on the car door as I hopped in each morning to begin another full day. The car was a constant reminder of the tremendous gift that I had received when I won the title of Miss Wisconsin. But it was also a subtle hint that all too soon my year would come to an end, and I'd have to turn the car over to the next lucky "Miss Wis." This made me want to pack everything in that I could now and really put to work "the power of the crown"!

Every day — even the bad ones! — was a pleasure. Yes, the physical and emotional demands of the job were taxing, but those paled in comparison with the tremendous rewards of the job. The students' response was almost always so positive and enthusiastic that I knew God's hand was upon them and the Holy Spirit was touching their hearts in a special way. It's difficult to express the joy and fulfillment that come when you leave a group of several hundred students knowing that most of them have been touched.

This surprises many people, especially skeptical adults who are out of touch with teens today. Eric Zorn, an editorial writer for the *Chicago Tribune*, stated in an anti-abstinence column that the expectation that young people will wait until marriage for sex "goes beyond folklore into fantasy." My response to him would be, "When was the last time you were in a high school?" He, like all too many adults, probably gets his information about teens from MTV videos and television sitcoms. But that's not reality — that's entertainment.

The reality is that *the majority of fifteen- to nineteen-year-olds in America are virgins* — fifty-three percent, according to a recent study. And this statistic doesn't include a large percentage of young people who have been sexually active in the past but have made the commitment to a "secondary virginity," not having sex again until marriage.

Volunteers Get Pushy

When I recall experiences that were typical of my year, Rockford Lutheran High School comes to mind. I visited this school in Illinois during a tour of four cities over three days. The tour was organized and sponsored by Stateline Life Advocates, a pro-life group on the border of Wisconsin and Illinois.

My schedule was extremely tight because of time constraints, and my first presentation of the day — a school assembly for Rockford Christian School — ended late.

I arrived at Rockford Lutheran literally moments before I was scheduled to begin. The principal and the guidance counselor met me at the door, looking relieved. "Welcome! They're all ready for you!" I hurried into the school with my umbrella (it rained incessantly during those three days), grabbed a roll of duct tape from my briefcase (I use it for an exercise I do with volunteers), clipped on the crown in the hallway using a trophy case window for reflection, and walked into the gym where almost eight hundred exuberant high school students filled both walls of bleachers and the chairs on the floor.

The students' initial attitude was typical — they were cheerfully skeptical. But by the end of my presentation, they were so excited about chastity that I had to pause frequently and ask them to stop cheering so much! Some of the senior guys, in their eagerness to volunteer for my duct tape example, actually knocked over the chairs of people sitting in front of them to try to run up to the front! (When this happens, I call it "self-appointed volunteers.")

As a reward for volunteering, these macho guys were allowed to choose from a variety of T-shirts provided by the Stateline Life Advocates. Each of the young men chose shirts that said, "Respect — I'm worth it!" and wore them proudly around school.

Other items that are very popular among students are the "True Love Waits" commitment cards and "I'm worth waiting for" stickers. Nonprofit groups often distribute these at schools and churches after my presentations. Students enjoy signing the cards and keeping them in their wallets or purses. They like to put the stickers on their backpacks, baseball caps, and even on their faces! It seems as if every time I go into a school, I find myself getting pumped up about chastity all over again!

Virgins Coming Out of the Closet!

I always enjoy addressing a portion of my presentation specifically to young men. Too often in society today, people think that while it's great for a woman to be pure, it's something that isn't important — or even admirable — in a man. I shoot down this myth by first discussing what really makes someone a man. I once heard Pam Stenzel say, "Having sex does *not* make you a man. Anybody can have sex! Animals have sex with each other all the time, right?" The kids always seem to get a kick out of this.

But then I seriously discuss with them some qualities that *do* make someone a man — character, integrity, self-respect, strength, courage, spirituality. "These are the things that make someone a man. And these are the things that I look for, that my friends look for, and that all of these young women here are looking for as well."

Sometimes a big revelation comes when I tell students, "There are a lot of young men in here who are virgins and who have already made this commitment to wait!" Many times, one or two guys stand up among their classmates and call out, "You got it! Right here!" or, "Yeah, that's right! That's me!" or even, "Yeah! Virgin and proud!"

I was totally taken by surprise the first time this happened. I was used to male audience members approaching me after a talk to tell me that they were virgins and were committed to chastity. But to stand up and broadcast it to hundreds of their classmates — this was an awesome display of courage that I had never dreamed of! Talk about "Standing With Courage"!

As this has become more common during my presentations, I've grown to understand it more. Just as people like to "come clean" and share very important, personal things with others, so do virgins — especially guys — want to tell others about their triumph over temptation! They're joyful about how they're taking on society with a rebellious, countercultural decision to live out high standards and choose the best in their lives.

Wearing His Heart on His Sleeve — I Mean Shirt

After a presentation at a church in a rural area, I was answering some private questions and signing baseball caps, T-shirts, etc., when a tall, handsome young man sat down next to me. Immediately about six or seven young women gathered around us. He told me that he was a senior at his high school and on the football team. And then he made an unusual request.

"Will you sign my shirt, and write 'virgin' in big letters on the back?"

The girls started laughing. Their commotion attracted about fifteen more guys and girls to our group.

"Sure!" I said. "I think that's really cool. But are you sure?"

"Absolutely," he said. "I'm proud of it!"

Then I had an idea. "Can I write something else, too?"

He looked at me, kind of surprised. "Well, okay, sure."

I wrote "V I R G I N" across the top of his shirt. Then underneath, I wrote, "And studly!"

The students roared with laughter. They started giving him high-fives. "He is so cool!" I heard one of the girls whisper. The young man got up and started to walk around the room to show everyone his shirt. "I think I'll wear this to school tomorrow," he said to me with a big smile.

The "new sexual revolution" is definitely catching on!

Making a New Beginning

Of course, not every teen or young adult wants to have "virgin" written across his back. And of course, not every teen or young adult is a virgin. Although the majority of teens today are, there are many who aren't. What about these students? Are they just left behind? Does chastity not apply to them?

No way! It's so important for such persons to know that no matter what they have done in the past, their sexuality is still a beautiful and precious gift! *They are still worth waiting for!* Although they might *feel* that their sexuality is worth less because they haven't treated it with the respect it deserves, all — young and old alike — need to know that their sexuality is valuable and beautiful. My friend, if this is your situation, you must know that *now is the time* to leave those destructive choices behind and make a new beginning!

I've heard all sorts of terms for this — secondary virginity, "born-again" virgins, even "recycled" virgins for the environmentally conscious! It doesn't matter what you call it — the point is the same: If you are a person who has had sex before marriage, no matter how many partners you've had, it's time for you to move to a higher level in your relationships. It's time for you to take a leap of faith. It's time for you to cast into deeper waters. It's time for you to leave your past behind and make a choice that comes with no regrets!

"The time has come to make a new beginning! . . ."

God of New Beginnings!

Jesus understands that we sometimes need a new beginning! Look at the parable of the Prodigal Son that He told His disciples. The Prodigal Son was about as bad as you can get. He had no respect for his family or friends. He even told his father to give him now what he was going to inherit when his father died — this by itself is very unfeeling and rude! Then he took the money and traveled to a foreign country where he squandered it all on drinking, prostitutes, and a very selfish, dissipated life. Eventually, he ran out of money and had to make his living taking care of pigs, an animal considered unclean in his Jewish faith. He was so poor that he couldn't afford to buy food and was so hungry that he longed to eat what the pigs ate.

Then the Prodigal Son finally came to his senses and realized what he had done. Even his father's slaves lived much better than he was living! The Prodigal Son knew that he was unworthy after betraying and abandoning his family, so he decided that he would get on his knees and ask his father for forgiveness, requesting that his father allow him to be one of the slaves.

> I will arise and go to my father, and I will say to him, "Father, I have sinned against heaven and before you; I am no longer worthy to be called your son; treat me as one of your hired servants."
>
> — LUKE 15:18-19

But his father would hear nothing of it.

> The father said to his servants, "Bring quickly the best robe, and put it on him; and put a ring on his hand, and shoes on his feet; and bring the fatted calf and kill it, and let us eat and make merry; for this my son was dead, and is alive again; he was lost, and is found."
>
> — LUKE 15:22-24

The father lovingly welcomed his son back with great joy! He completely forgave him and gave his son the freedom to make a new beginning!

Have you been lost up to this point? Have your choices been causing something inside of you to die — your self-respect, purity, and longing to be loved unconditionally? Are you giving yourself the forgiveness and freedom to make a new beginning in your own life?

It's time to stop beating yourself up for past mistakes. You can't change the past, but a future of promise awaits you! The saving power of God's love is awesome! He is calling you by name! He is inviting you to leave your past life at the foot of the Cross and to embrace the new life that He has waiting for you!

God wants to put a chastity ring on your finger and clothe you again in purity! He wants you to come home and reclaim your joy and freedom through chastity! He lovingly invites you to make a new beginning!

This isn't a decision to be taken lightly. Before the Prodigal Son could come home and start over, he had to take a good look at himself. He had to face the facts and admit his guilt. The same is true for you. If you want to make a new beginning and you've been making unchaste choices up to this point, you have to acknowledge that what you did was wrong. You must confess that you regret those choices. And then, you'll be ready to move to a higher level in your life. After taking these steps, you can truly "cast out into deeper waters" and make the commitment to chastity. I guarantee that once you start down this path of self-respect, spirituality, and empowerment, you will never look back!

Reclaiming Their Purity

A young woman approached me after a presentation at a public high school in a small Wisconsin town and said, "I've had sex with a lot of guys, but I'd always been drunk, so I didn't think it mattered. Now I realize that I gave each of those guys a special part of myself. I don't want all that pain and hurt anymore. I'm going to make a new beginning and not have sex again until I'm married."

Another girl from an urban public high school told me, "I was really in love with this guy and I gave myself to him, and then he just dumped me. And I felt so bad about it that I couldn't get over him. I thought if I just did the same things with someone else, I'd forget about him. So I had sex with all these other guys, too. But in the end, I felt worse — like I'd been used, like I was cheap. I didn't know what to do. I thought I had to keep doing it, because I'd already done it so many times. But after hearing you, I feel happy, because I've decided that from now on I'm going to start a secondary virginity and I'm going to wait until I'm married. I feel like my body is worth something again."

A young man at a technical college came up to me after a presentation and said, "You've forced me to take a good look at my life. I realize now that some of the choices I've been making aren't the best. I need to start over. I'm going to change my life starting today."

The Faces Behind the Statistics

Unfortunately, not every story has a happy ending. After a presentation at a Christian school in a small town, a freshman girl approached me, choking back tears. "I'm a virgin, but I have genital herpes," she confided. "No one told me that you can get it just by touch." She had been in a relationship with an older man who had introduced her to a lot of sexual experiences. She didn't know much about his past, she said, but she never suspected that he had an STD. Because they didn't have intercourse, she thought that she was "safe." She was unaware that some of the most common sexually transmitted diseases like herpes and HPV are passed through skin contact, which is how she contracted genital herpes. She said to me, "I'd be doing what you're doing if I could. But I can't. So I want you to tell my story wherever you go, so that others don't make the same mistake I did."

The Disease of Low Expectations

At a middle school in a rural area of Wisconsin, an eighth-grader arranged to meet with me after a presentation. She was pregnant. The baby's father was a high school student and he made it clear that he didn't want anything to do with her or their baby. The girl said that her mother had been very support-ive. "My mother had me in kind of the same situation," she said, "so she understands. She said that she knew it was just a matter of time anyway before I did the same thing that she did."

I was deeply saddened to hear this. Her mother never be-lieved that she would have the self-respect or self-control to wait. In fact, she *expected* her daughter to get pregnant outside marriage. By getting pregnant in the eighth grade, this girl was merely fulfilling her mother's expectations. She had the poten-tial to do so much more — and to be so much more. This girl had many talents and gifts yet to be developed! But because of her mother's low expectations, she will never achieve what she could have in her life. Instead, she now has to cope with the loneliness and struggles of being a thirteen-year-old single mother in a small town.

This young woman is a vivid example of how important it is to expect the best, both from yourself and others. High expec-tations help us to believe in ourselves, set high goals, and achieve our dreams! My friend, never allow other people to set low expectations for you. You were created to accomplish great things in your life!

For my generation, the standard was set so low that we had to crawl through the gutter to get to the other side. In the pro-cess, hundreds of thousands of young people, including some of my close friends, suffered some painful, lifelong consequences. They weren't given the chance to bring their light to the world and to achieve their mission.

What if, instead of having such low expectations of teens and young adults, our society held us to high standards? What if, instead of glorifying premarital sex, our society discouraged it? I think many lives would be a lot different today. And I think we would see the results throughout our society — fewer out-of-wedlock pregnancies, fewer people with STDs, fewer women and children living in poverty, and more happy marriages.

Invincible Hope!

But sometimes even the most hopeless situations can be filled with promise! I spoke at an inner-city middle school in an area plagued by unemployment, drug use, and crime. Teen pregnancy was rampant; there were day-care centers in all of the high schools, and one high school had an abortion clinic across the street. Almost all of the students at this middle school came from single-parent families, often with situations of abuse and addiction. Most of the students participated in government-funded school breakfast and lunch programs, and their families were on welfare.

When I walked into the school, the principal immediately rushed me into the gym. It was the end of the school day, and we were on a tight schedule. "The only way we could fit all of our students into the same room was to have them sit in the bleachers on all four sides of the gym. So you'll have to do it kind of 'in the round,' " she said. "I hope you don't mind."

"This is going to be interesting!" I thought. I had never done this before. But for some reason, a wave of energy and excitement was welling up inside of me. I had only about twenty-five minutes to touch these students' hearts. How would I cut down an hour-long presentation into such a short period of time? I had no idea — but I knew that the Holy Spirit would guide me.

As I began, I looked into the faces of these students, so tough, so insecure, but so filled with hope! They knew about suffering, much more than your average eleven- to fourteen-year-olds. They knew the pain of broken families and shattered dreams. But then it hit me — *they also knew that there must be something better out there!*

I started by talking about their dreams, goals, the things that they want to do in their lives and how they must dream big! They must create a vision of the life they want, not based on what's around them, but what is inside of them! And then, they can take action to make it happen! I said, "No matter what kind of situation you come from, no matter what kinds of problems are happening at home, no matter what kind of family you're in, each of you can make the right choices, and you can achieve your dreams!" At this, the students started cheering and clapping. I emphasized to them the importance of the choices that they make, and I shared with them the meaning of the choices I made, especially abstinence until marriage. When I told them that I was a virgin, they actually broke into enthusiastic applause!

I remembered that many of these students were from broken homes and needed love. I said, "You know, one thing that all of us have in common is that *all of us want to be loved* in a lifelong, meaningful, exciting way. And all of us want to give love in this way, too! Then we go out there in the world, and what do we see? We see that about one out of two marriages ends in divorce. We see people who don't even believe in marriage or who think that a good marriage is random, just like rolling the dice. It's like, 'Let's see if I luck out and I get a good marriage.' So what's the point of waiting, you might think, if your marriage is going to break up anyway?"

A hush fell over the gym as the students listened attentively. Four hundred young faces looked at me inquisitively, expectantly, searching for the answer. This was the question that was within each of their hearts, the key to unlock the mystery, the sadness, the meaning of their lives. Was there something better out there? Perhaps no one had ever talked with them about this before.

And to tell you the truth, I had never talked about this before myself! I was winging it, but it was the inspiration of the Holy Spirit guiding me through.

"The good news is that each of you — no matter what your parents are like, no matter whether you even have parents, no matter what you've done in your past — each of you has the ability to have a lifetime, loving, exciting, romantic, joyful marriage!" The gymnasium buzzed. A few of them cheered, "Yeah!" "All right!"

I went on, "But you've got to do two things. First, you've got to prepare yourself. Do you have the self-control to be faithful to someone for a lifetime? That's why abstinence is so important, because it prepares you.

"And second, you've got to choose your spouse well. Those people out there who are living together or having sex before marriage — does that help them to choose well? Or are they so involved with the sex that they can't really see things clearly? That's why abstinence before marriage is so important! I don't care what you've done in your past! Each of you is worth waiting for!"

The students erupted into cheers and applause and started stomping on the bleachers! They quieted down as I shared with them the song "Walk a Little Slower, My Friend," which made such a great impact on my life at their age and, at the end, they jumped to their feet and clapped wildly. After calming them down, I said, "So, are you going to join Miss Wisconsin in not having sex until marriage?" And four hundred-some students took to their feet again, shouting, *"Yes!"* Their cheers were almost deafening as they threw their arms in the air and gave each other high-fives!

The principal was speechless. Every single student in that gym was on fire with a zeal for purity, truth, and meaning in his or her life! After the students settled down, she said, "This is incredible. You students have shown me something very special today — you've given all of us teachers and faculty something very special, something I don't think any of us will forget. I hope you always remember this moment. I hope you always remember Miss Wisconsin's message. If you put her words into practice, this day could change your life forever."

Those students deeply touched my heart. Their enthusiasm and excitement, and especially their invincible hope — these are what inspire me most. They have an unquenchable flame in their hearts that continues to burn, in spite of the tough challenges that life has given them.

Whenever I get discouraged or feel apprehensive about accepting a request to speak in a dangerous area, I remember those kids. Every child deserves to hear this message. Every child needs to know that, no matter what kind of family situation such children come from or how much money they have, they can find lasting love in their lives — and they can achieve their dreams.

12

In the Lion's Den

Behold, I send you out as sheep in the midst of wolves; so be
wise as serpents and innocent as doves.

— MATTHEW 10:16

Sometimes in life, things can be tough. We have to go to places
that we don't want to go to and do things we don't want to do.
We have to take the risk of standing up for what is right when
other people are taking the easy way out. We're called to be *rebels
for truth*.

It's not easy to stay true to your convictions, especially if you
believe in something that isn't very popular. I'm sure you've had
experiences where people have teased you, embarrassed you, or
ridiculed you for doing what is right. Sometimes it's hard to
speak up for truth.

Most of my experiences as Miss Wisconsin were incredibly
joyful, but there were times when things got very tough. I encountered criticism from the media, opposition from abortion
advocates, skepticism from school administrators, hostility from
reporters, and even condescension from talk show hosts. These
adults had a difficult time understanding my work and the reality of the "new sexual revolution" that is sweeping across the
United States.

During these moments of attack, I sometimes felt like Daniel
in the lion's den! So I tried to emulate his example by trusting
completely in God's love to keep me safe and help me be effective in these unfriendly environments. In the process, I learned
more fully what it means to stand with courage.

Madison Students Get Mad

A few days before speaking at the University of Wisconsin, I received a distraught phone call from one of the leaders of the group that was sponsoring my presentation. The event organizer, "Karen," said that some students had threatened to protest the event. They said that they were not only planning to demonstrate outside but would come into the hall where I was speaking to disrupt my presentation and "take over." These students suggested that the group cancel, "to avoid any confrontations that might arise."

When I heard this, I knew that cancellation was not an option. These people wanted to prevent the truth from being spoken on their campus, where this message was desperately needed! I was determined that they would not succeed in suppressing the truth. It reminded me of the passage from Isaiah that inspired me so much at the Miss America Pageant:

> For Zion's sake I will not keep silent,
>> and for Jerusalem's sake I will not rest,
> until her vindication goes forth as brightness,
>> and her salvation as a burning torch.
>
> — ISAIAH 62:1

For the sake of those students, I could not surrender to fear and keep silent! This mission was unstoppable!

When I arrived in Madison, I noticed signs and posters all over campus advertising my presentation. Some had been defaced with graffiti, with words like *"Repressed"* written across my picture. When I arrived at the hall to speak, there was hardly anyone there. Karen welcomed me warmly and apologized for the small turnout. "I guess the protesters kept people away," she sighed. I told her not to worry about it, remembering how busy I was in college. It's difficult to get college students to any forum, especially when the topic is considered to be so "uncool" on campus.

There were about sixty people in the audience when I began. About twenty minutes later, the protesters burst into the back of the room, holding signs and posters and making plenty of noise. I continued as if nothing had happened, pretending that they didn't exist. They watched me angrily, talking among themselves and gesturing forcefully. One of them tried to interrupt me several times, but I simply looked at him and continued.

Then I noticed that there were a number of young women among their group. "How can these girls be so out of touch?" I wondered to myself. "Could they think that premarital sex is empowering?" Trashing my original presentation, I decided to "cut to the chase" and expose how unloving and selfish these unchaste guys really are. Using some wisdom from Pam Stenzel, I said, "Ladies, if a young man says to you, 'I love you — you need to prove that you love me. If you love me, you'll have sex with me' . . . think about what this guy is saying! He's not saying 'I love you!' He's saying, 'I *hormone* you. . . .' " The students laughed as I continued, "And he's saying, 'I want you to meet my momentary desire.' Young women, *real love* wouldn't ask you to put your life, your dreams, or your future at risk to meet his momentary desire! Real love respects. And real love waits!"

The protesters quieted down and left a few minutes later. I hope that those young women went off to think about what I said. As for the guys, they probably didn't want the girls to hear any more about chastity, lest they be held to a higher standard!

The remainder of the presentation went off without a hitch, and the question-and-answer session at the end was especially good. The students' enthusiasm and insights about bringing chastity into dating generated a great discussion. Karen approached me with a relieved smile. "It went great! I'm so glad nothing happened! When I saw that group come in, my heart was pounding. They were really trying to start something; but you were so cool, you just kept right on going. I bet some people didn't even notice them!"

I wasn't the one who kept those protesters from getting out of hand — it was the power of the Holy Spirit! Whatever they had planned, I knew that there was very little I could do about it. But I only needed to do one thing — trust in Jesus.

> The LORD is my light and my salvation;
>   whom shall I fear?
> The LORD is the stronghold of my life;
>   of whom shall I be afraid?
>
> — PSALM 27:1

'Politically Incorrect' a Little Too Correct for Me

My experience at the University of Wisconsin-Madison was one of many intimidating situations I encountered through my work speaking about chastity. The most challenging by far was my first appearance on ABC's *Politically Incorrect with Bill Maher*. A few months after the Madison experience, I found myself in the Green Room of CBS studios in Los Angeles with three Hollywood celebrities looking into the "trial by fire" that surely awaited me as I faced down the show's popular host on national television.

Bill Maher is one of my favorite people to pray for. Someday, he could become a great saint! If you know who he is, you may think he's a pretty unlikely subject. Even though he was raised Catholic and Jewish (his parents' religions) his show can be quite crude, even offensive at times. In fact, one of my friends suggested that his show should be called "Nothing Sacred" instead of "Politically Incorrect"! Bill has many natural, God-given gifts — sharp intelligence, keen insightfulness, and a quick sense of humor. His fast-paced half-hour show is taped in front of a live audience, and he brings on a panel of four guests for each program to debate various political and cultural issues. The twist is that three of the guests usually hold more liberal opinions and they all gang up on a fourth, more conservative guest. Sometimes they get into pretty heated debates. Bill is a skilled debater who loves to poke fun at everything and everyone! Some of his favorite issues are drug legalization, making fun of Christians, and picking on George W. Bush.

My friends and family were quite concerned when I agreed to be a guest on P.I. They knew that I was going to be made fun of and criticized. My work with teens and my lifestyle would be a perfect vehicle for Bill and his other guests to make some jokes and get laughs from the audience. I had turned down requests to appear on other programs like *Queen Latifah* and *Dr. Joy Browne*. Why had I accepted this gig, when I knew that they were just going to make a mockery of me?

I had considered this decision for several months, so I was aware of what I was getting into. Why did I go through with it? In my heart, I felt that God was asking me to bring my message to *this* audience, an audience that desperately needs to hear about chastity from someone who is "in touch" with the world and living a mainstream life. So many people in their twenties, thirties, and forties try to find happiness through superficial relationships and loveless sex. Many suffer serious physical and emotional consequences from those choices.

What if they discovered the freedom, joy, empowerment, and great relationships that come with chastity? That would be awesome! God wants to speak to their hearts — and to invite them home! I felt that if I could help even one person to make a change of heart, being humiliated on national television was a small sacrifice!

This is what Jesus did in His life — he "infiltrated" the mainstream culture and reached out to everyone. He didn't hang out only with people who agreed with Him or who had a strong faith. He went to those who needed Him most, from tax collectors to fishermen, from prostitutes to the well-to-do. Everyone was included in His work and everyone who was open to His love found freedom and healing.

Battle at the Front Line

The topics for the show were faxed to me beforehand. (These actually changed drastically once we were "on the air.") But I didn't have any other idea of what was going to happen, other than from what I had seen on TV. I wondered, "Would I meet Bill before the show? Would the panel discuss the topics first, and then replay the discussion for the taping? Would we be directed to focus on certain cameras as we were talking? Will they tell us when they're cutting to a commercial?"

As I sat in the Green Room with the show's staff and the other guests, I realized that no one was going to spoon-feed me through this process. The show thrives on the spontaneous and unexpected — this is what entertains. As guests, our goal was to do or say anything that keeps people from switching the channel. My personal goal was a little more specific — to convey my message in an entertaining, but effective, way.

My friend Bob, who lives in Los Angeles, joined me in the Green Room beforehand to give me some moral support. I was exhausted! The day before was jam-packed, what with three presentations and about two hundred miles of driving. I had boarded an airplane that morning at about 5:00 Pacific Time and had to fly through Cincinnati to get from Milwaukee to Los Angeles, making my flight time even longer! After so many hours on a plane, I was ready for a good nap — not for a lively debate with four celebrities ganging up on me on national television!

If I hadn't been aware of my role as the punching-bag prior to arriving in L.A., the show's staff definitely would have clued me in. "Don't be afraid," one of the girls who worked for P.I. said to me condescendingly, trying to stifle a laugh. "It's all just for fun."

I smiled, thinking, "I'm not afraid — I have the Holy Spirit!"

I enjoyed getting to know the other guests and found some things in common with them. James Marsters, an actor on *Buffy the Vampire Slayer,* had studied theater at Julliard, a school I had looked at during my college search. Comedienne Nicole Sullivan from *Mad TV* was born in upstate New York, where I had lived for six years. Tray Deee, a rapper from the L.A. area, had recorded a lot of raps with offensive lyrics. Hm-m-m-m . . . Not too much common ground there! But it was good to "bond" with them by chatting a little before the show — we laid the foundation for great "on-camera chemistry."

And then, it was time. As I waited behind the set for my entrance, my heart was pounding so loudly that I could barely hear Bill's monologue. I knew that in this next half hour, I was set up to be the sacrificial lamb, and millions of people would be watching! "Holy Spirit, I put this completely in Your hands," I prayed. Then Bill was announcing my name, and I was running up three steps onto the set to meet him for the first time in front of a live audience of about a hundred fifty and a TV audience of some nine million people.

Bill started in on me right away. "You're a board-certified virgin," he joked. "Absolutely!" I responded. He said, "Well, we're not going to quibble about that, but your platform was abstinence." "It *is* abstinence, that's right," I said.

The studio audience laughed at me! I turned around with a smile and playfully stared them down, which got an even bigger laugh. Although the cameramen totally missed this for television, it was an important first move. It was my way of saying, "I'm ready for you, and I'm here to have some fun, too!"

As the show continued, the discussion took its expected course, fluctuating between "pageant-bashing" and "abstinence-bashing." Bill expressed his opinion that it's "unnatural" to be abstinent, and that "nature" directs what is truth. (If he truly believed this, he'd be a firm opponent of abortion, which is an extremely unnatural procedure!) I pointed out to him that we're not created to be like animals in the barnyard, where sex is just a physical act that should be done whenever we get the urge. Rather, our sexuality is something beautiful and precious — so precious that it's worth waiting for. I said, "I've had plenty of opportunities to have sex —"

Bill interrupted, "Well, no kidding, you're a chick!" The audience laughed.

I continued, "But I'm holding out for something more, for something better."

Tray Deee said, "Some nights, you just want to feel good!" This got a big laugh, and Bill said, "I couldn't have said it better myself."

I came back with the statistic that guarantees victory. "Actually, Tray, studies show that married people have the most pleasurable sex."

Bill discounted this, saying, "Well, studies lie! And married people lie!"

When I pointed out that the majority of teens are virgins, he replied, "That's because they can't get any!" What an untrue statement! But then again, when was the last time someone saw Bill Maher in a high school?

The other guests were very nice to me, but they, the audience, and Bill seemed to regard me as an amusing and pathetic character.

After the show, I felt pretty beaten. Bob tried to cheer me up over dinner, but I couldn't stop thinking about what had just happened. My goal was to show people that chastity is a "hip" and rewarding lifestyle, but instead I thought I had made things worse! "Maybe it would have been better if I had never gone on the show at all!" I thought.

Fortunately, the broadcast was much better than I expected. Phone calls and e-mails poured in from friends. "You did a great job! You were awesome! Way to go!" I really appreciated all of their support, even if it was biased. Even strangers e-mailed the Miss Wisconsin website with lots of positive comments. It definitely had been a "lion's den" experience, but the Holy Spirit sustained me through it all!

'Politically Incorrect' Strikes Again

Last September, after my year as Miss Wisconsin had ended, I received another invitation to be a guest on P.I. I leaped at the opportunity. Now that I knew what to expect, I felt I'd be better prepared. And I was eager to get into some deeper topics than those on the previous show. Most importantly, I was really yearning to share my testimony — I wanted to tell the world that my commitment to chastity is the best choice I've ever made in my life. Who can argue with that?

But when I received the topics for the program, I realized that sharing my testimony wouldn't be possible with these issues — unless something really extraordinary happened. The other guests were actor Jay Thomas, novelist Elmore Leonard, and *Playboy* model Summer Altice. Things were definitely going to be interesting.

As I stood behind the set, my heart was really pounding, but this time for different reasons. My trip to L.A. was a disaster, causing me to arrive at the studio only ten minutes before the taping! I was going on national television in front of nine million people, and I didn't even know if I was going to be ready in time, much less prepare myself for the heated debate that was sure to follow. Yikes! As I tried to take my mind off of these silly but alarming ideas, I looked up, and there were Mom and Dad sitting across from me in the audience, looking right at me and giving me the "thumbs up"!

Seeing them restored my confidence. I remembered that this time I was on familiar turf. I was ready. The Holy Spirit was with me. I thought of the *Star Wars* theme to get myself "pumped up" for the battle ahead. The Force was with me! Little did I know that in just a few seconds I'd have the most embarrassing moment of my life.

Embarrassment to the Max!

Bill Maher introduced me the way he always does, with my entrance cue, "There she is, Mary-Louise Kurey! Mary!" I enthusiastically ran up the three steps with a big smile on my face, and *tripped!*

Could it be true? I laughed at my klutziness and caught myself right away, but it was still undoubtedly a trip, something nine million people would see! And then, I saw a wonderful side of Bill — he was actually sympathetic and forgiving to a conservative! "Good to see you again!" he said, giving me a smile and a kiss on the cheek. Then he added, "I've almost done that myself a few times!" I was surprised and grateful that he was so nice about it.

During the first break, I said, "Bill, can you believe I did that?"

"Did what?" he said, looking up from his cards.

"I tripped!"

"Oh, don't worry about it — it wasn't that bad! You know, I've had nightmares about doing that myself!" he confessed with a smile.

There are few people more opposite than Bill Maher and I. But at that moment, we found common ground — we share the same feelings of embarrassment, the same fears. We disagree on almost everything, but still are able to understand and respect each other.

Unexpected Opportunity!

Jay Thomas and I, on the other hand, were like oil and water! At the beginning of the show, we got into a pretty hot debate over school choice, a program that is very successful in Milwaukee, but which he opposes. When the topic turned to college girls' insecurities when it comes to sex, he became very rude. Everyone was talking at once, and then he shouted in a mocking tone, "Wait a minute! We haven't heard what *the virgin* has to say!"

I thought, "Here's my chance!" He played right into my hand!

"That's right," I said. "I am a virgin, I've made the commitment to wait until marriage, and it's the best choice I've ever made in my life." And then, something incredible happened. The whole audience applauded — including the *Playboy* model!

Bill looked stunned by the audience's reaction. When the clapping and cheers died down, he said, "It's a sad perversion, but go on."

"Right back at ya!" I responded.

He laughed and shrugged his shoulders.

Summer compared sex to driving a car. "Don't you have to try it out first, to know if you're compatible with someone?" she asked. "No," I responded firmly. I explained that people are a lot different from cars. If someone feels he has to "try me out" before deciding to marry me, then obviously that person doesn't love me.

Jay said to Summer, "You'd be like driving a Ferrari for me!" She smiled, not really looking happy, and I felt badly that this older man would say something so degrading to her on national television. Little did I know what he was cooking up for me! I protested, and he turned to me and said, "All right, let's hear what the VW Beetle has to say."

"You're still sore about that school choice thing," I said with a smile, patting his hand.

The final topic was the movie *The Exorcist*, which was about to be rereleased. Bill and Jay contended that religions exist just to frighten people and that the Catholic Church wanted people to think that *The Exorcist* was real. I pointed out that although there are a small number of real cases of demonic possession, *The Exorcist* was never intended to be realistic and it certainly wasn't made or condoned by the Catholic Church. It's just entertainment! Bill doubted the existence of the devil. "Oh, come on, Bill!" I said. "There is so much evil in the world!"

"I know," he acknowledged. "But why does it have to be done by a devil?"

I was delighted. Bill had acknowledged the existence of evil on national television! He was really coming along! The prayers were already showing results! Except for my tripping, the show went well. After the show, Bill gave me a kiss on the cheek and said, "Excellent job as always." I told him that it was a pleasure to be on his show again and thanked him for the opportunity.

These experiences — Madison, *Politically Incorrect*, and many others — were a true test of my faith and courage. They taught me that I should never be afraid to speak out or stay true to my beliefs, because God will always be there to help me.

My friend, the same is true for you! God will always be with you to help you stand strong and "be a rebel for truth" as you carry out your mission! The only thing that He asks in return is your love — and the willingness to stand with courage. With these things, you and your mission will be *unstoppable*.

13

An Epiphany of Love!

Sometimes people ask, "What was your favorite experience as Miss Wisconsin?"

There are a lot of great possibilities: my work with teens, my experiences at Miss America, the conferences and events I spoke at, meeting important and famous people. But among all of these wonderful experiences, there is one that stands out: being on the television show *Life on the Rock* (LOTR for short). On that show, I experienced a beautiful personal transformation. It was truly an "epiphany," a leap to a new level in my understanding of love and chastity, and what life really is all about.

LOTR Junkie

I had watched LOTR for about three years and had become a huge fan. The issues that were discussed on the show were very relevant to my life, especially when I was thirsting for spiritual friendships as a graduate student at Duquesne. I had a few Catholic friends in Pittsburgh who were somewhat excited about their faith, and I was yearning to be nourished and guided in my walk with Christ. The guests on LOTR were very inspiring. But most of all, I was incredibly moved by the show's dynamic host, Jeff Cavins!

Jeff has such zeal, and he really loves God and others so much! As I watch his show week after week, I always feel the Holy Spirit moving within him and reaching out to his viewers. What impresses me most is how much he is "in touch" with the world. He understands the temptations and struggles that teens and young adults encounter today. He also has a great knowledge of Scripture and the Catholic faith — and he delivers his message with awesome charisma!

I remember the first time I watched *Life on the Rock*. I cried when it ended, and I didn't even know why! It just was really cool! The theme song by Joe and Jeanne Ann Hand spoke to me in a powerful way.

> *This is your life, whether you're ready or not.*
> *Sometimes it's rough, and it takes all that you've got.*
> *But He's been here, just waiting for you to knock,*
> *So take His hand, and plant your feet on the Rock!*
> *I want to live my life on the Rock . . .*

At the time, I was feeling so overwhelmed in my life. I was balancing an enormous workload, tight finances, and departmental politics. In my work, I had been forced to witness a side of people that I never wanted to see, and I faced some tough decisions. When I heard this song, something that had been buried inside of me was awakened — the need to surrender my life fully to God, so He could show me the way and give me strength and courage to do the right thing. Jeff's show guided and inspired me through these difficult times. I looked forward to it every Thursday night.

When I was invited to be a guest on LOTR, I was thrilled! But as the date neared, I became terrified! The guests were always so holy, and I'm not even close to their level of spirituality. But I reminded myself that God was giving me another very special opportunity to reach teens and young adults with His beautiful message of love.

My parents and I arrived in Birmingham the night before the show and were able to be in the studio audience for *Mother Angelica Live*. It was exciting to watch the production of a live show that is broadcast to five continents! Mother Angelica was mobbed with people after the program, but she took the time to say hello and have a picture with me. I also met a lot of other impressive people that I had seen on TV, including Raymond Arroyo, the host of *The World Over* and *EWTN Newslink*.

The next day, we attended Mass at the monastery, and I walked around the EWTN grounds. I was really nervous, but I found peace as I prayed before the Blessed Sacrament and meditated on the Stations of the Cross in the garden. It was wonderful to take in the marvel that God had created through the work of a single nun with a dream.

Complete Preparation?

I couldn't wait to meet Jeff in person that afternoon! I was especially anxious to discuss specifics about the show. Jeff greeted my parents and me warmly, then took us on a tour of the EWTN facilities, including the set for *Life on the Rock*. It looked a lot smaller when I saw it in person! We did a sound-check before having dinner at the Madonna House, one of the residences on the EWTN campus, where I met Alice von Hildebrand. I was really enjoying myself, but I kept wondering when we were going to discuss the show. Time was going by quickly. Jeff said to me, "I'm going to take you back to your hotel to get ready for the show. Is forty minutes enough?"

"Aren't we going to go over the show?" I asked, trying not to sound nervous.

Jeff was very relaxed. "You've talked about this topic a lot. I don't think we need to go over anything. I'll ask you some questions about yourself and your experiences at Miss America, and then we'll talk about chastity and your work with teens," he said very casually. "It's going to be great!"

About an hour later, I found myself praying with Jeff in Mother Angelica's office, moments before the broadcast. I prayed that the Holy Spirit would inspire me to say the things that people watching needed to hear. I prayed that He would touch their hearts.

The Coffeehouse That Rocks

The live audience was packed, from the tables in the "coffeehouse" to the bleachers in front of the "performance space" where I would sing. The lights were up, the cameras were ready, the audience was waiting, and the countdown was on. As the cameras started to roll, Jeff said to his international audience, "If you had the opportunity to stand up in front of the country, like at the Miss America Pageant, what would you say? We'll find out what one young woman said, next on *Life on the Rock*."

And then came that incredible LOTR theme song: *"This is your life, whether you're ready or not . . ."* As I heard those words, I had a flashback from a year before, when I was a graduate assistant sitting alone in my apartment watching *Life on the Rock*. It was hard to believe that I was now a guest on the show I had loved for so long! My life had changed so completely!

I felt tears of gratitude welling up, and I looked at my parents, who were sitting in the front row of the bleachers. My mother's expression was one I've seen often in important moments — serene, contemplative. She was praying. My dad, on the other hand, looked terrified! He was clutching Mom's hand with an iron grip! I couldn't help but laugh, and it helped me shake the tears a few moments before my song.

As Jeff and I talked about my life and the work I was doing with teens, I realized for the first time that my chaotic, unexpected life, with all of its quirky twists and turns, really had taken shape into a wonderful direction under God's care. Many of my dreams had gone unfulfilled — becoming Miss America, being an Olympic track star, performing leading roles on Broadway. My life had turned out a lot differently from what I had planned. But God's plan was so much better! His dreams for me, His "surprise mission," had brought me more joy and fulfillment than I ever could have imagined!

Chastity Recap!

In the midst of this joy, as I shared with Jeff about chastity and its role in my life, something was happening inside of me. I had spent years telling people why chastity is terrific in tangible, easy-to-see reasons that the world can understand. The world can grasp these reasons, analyze them, and dissect them into sound bytes for the evening news if necessary.

My friend, I hope that by now you also know these reasons for chastity and have made them your own, thinking about how you can tell these to your friends based on what is important to you. You might remember that at the beginning of the book, I organized my three motivations for chastity into three priorities: "The Three F's"— My Family, My Future, and My Faith. In case you're still trying to decide which reasons for chastity are most important to you, here's a quick rundown:

- The *personal benefits of chastity:* strength, perseverance, self-respect, integrity, courage, high standards, a life based on truth, and a strong, open relationship with God.
- The *social benefits of chastity:* a great dating life, more exciting and healthier relationships, friends who share high standards, and a better understanding of what male-female relationships are all about.
- The *avoidance of negative consequences:* sexually transmitted diseases, painful emotional scars, spiritual isolation, and pregnancy outside marriage.
- The *goal-oriented benefits of chastity:* preparation for an awesome marriage or vocation, empowerment to achieve your dreams, and the freedom to discover your personal mission to bring to the world.

And there are many, many more reasons for chastity, which I'm sure you can think of right off the top of your head!

What's Happening?

These reasons had always satisfied me. I believed in them — and I lived them out. I knew that they were real. But somehow, they suddenly weren't enough. I felt like there was something else, a larger picture that I was missing.

It was something having to do with that *feeling* I got in seventh grade when I first made the commitment to chastity. When I decided that I would live out a chaste lifestyle, an amazing warmth, peacefulness, and fulfillment enfolded me — a sense of not quite understanding what I had just done but knowing that I had just done something very right. Here I was, thirteen years later, sitting on a live TV program broadcast all over the world engaged in a great discussion, secretly asking myself, "What am I missing? Have I lost the forest in the midst of the trees?"

Mary's Gift

In spite of my inner distractions, the show went well, and it was now time for me to wrap up with two songs, starting with the "Ave Maria." But what was this question nagging at my heart? Why now, of all times, was I feeling the need to analyze, to search for something deeper in my commitment to chastity? I should have been focusing on preparing to sing, but I couldn't help but listen to those questions that were causing my heart to pound for some mysterious reason!

I began the song, trusting that Mary would help me through my silly distractions.

Ave Maria, gratia plena,	*Hail Mary, full of grace,*
Dominus tecum.	*The Lord is with thee.*
Benedicta tu in mulieribus,	*Blessed art thou among women,*
Et benedictus fructus ventris tui, Iesus.	*And blessed is the fruit of thy womb, Jesus.*
Sancta Maria, Mater Dei,	*Holy Mary, Mother of God,*

Ora pro nobis peccatoribus   *Pray for us sinners,*
Nunc et in hora mortis nostrae. Amen.   *Now and at the hour of our*
                                                                          death. Amen.

As I sang, I surrendered my questions to Mary, who is truly the Queen of Chastity, the ultimate role model, the only person (besides Jesus, who was also God's Son) who was totally without sin. She lived a life of incredible purity, with a heart as loving and immaculate as anyone could ever imagine. As I sang, I contemplated her Immaculate Heart, her tender love for Jesus, and her love for each of her sons and daughters — that's you and me! As I thought about her life, the ocean of mystery parted, and I saw the big picture.

Crossing the Ocean of Understanding

Then Moses stretched out his hand over the sea; and the LORD drove the sea back by a strong east wind all night, and made the sea dry land, and the waters were divided. And the people of Israel went into the midst of the sea on dry ground, the waters being a wall to them on their right hand and on their left. The Egyptians pursued, and went in after them into the midst of the sea, all Pharaoh's horses, his chariots, and his horsemen.

Then the LORD said to Moses, "Stretch out your hand over the sea, that the water may come back upon the Egyptians, upon their chariots, and upon their horsemen." So Moses stretched forth his hand over the sea, and the sea returned to its wonted flow when the morning appeared; and the Egyptians fled into it, and the LORD routed the Egyptians in the midst of the sea. The waters returned and covered the chariots and the horsemen and all the host of Pharaoh that had followed them into the sea; not so much as one of them remained.

— EXODUS 14:21-23, 26-28

When Moses led the Israelites out of Egypt, they knew about the Red Sea. They were familiar with it growing up — it wasn't that far away from where they lived. They even camped next to it that night. But they had no idea what it looked like on the other side. When Pharaoh's army came after them, any possibility of escape looked hopeless. Then God intervened with an amazing, supernatural solution. He parted the waters of this enormous sea, giving the Israelites a view of their mission, their destination across the sea that they had never seen. They were freed from slavery and on track to continue their mission.

I was very familiar with chastity, from living it out each day. I thought I understood it pretty well, by thinking about it and analyzing it just like the world did. But God helped me to raise my understanding to a new level, to give me a greater vision of the big picture. He parted the sea through the tangible, concrete reasons for chastity, the ideas that I had been familiar with for so long. I saw that these things are part of a much larger picture of why chastity is so important. I had been very focused on the beauty of the trees — the concrete reasons for chastity. But the forest — the larger purpose of chastity — is far more breathtaking and amazing than I had ever imagined!

Chastity goes *way beyond* those!

The Mission Is Love!

Mary's life showed me that chastity is an intrinsic part of *loving* — loving God, others, and myself! When people talk about love in our society, they're usually talking about something that is primarily self-serving. Movies, TV shows, and music usually portray relationships of "love" as being rooted in sex, with two people who need each other to feel complete. Relationships of "love" in high school and college are often about, "Who am I most attracted to?" "Who gives me status?" or, "Who makes me feel good about myself?"

These things aren't bad, but they're not nearly so great as the *reality* of *real love*. Real love is giving from your heart completely for another person, putting aside your own wishes, and making that person your number one priority after loving God. And through this tremendous giving, you receive more than you could ever imagine! I realized that real love requires sacrifice, just as Christ made the ultimate sacrifice for you and me.

Living Out Chastity Is Intrinsic to Love, the Purpose of Our Lives!

I realized that I had been transformed: Chastity was no longer a burden, something I grudgingly did because God asked me to, while I listed all of the good reasons for it. I discovered that I was living chastity not out of obligation, but out of *love!*

I had come on the show to minister to others, but God used the show to minister to me! I realized that my year hadn't only been about bringing the message of chastity to others. It had been *a journey of love*, a mission of light that was greater than anything I had ever envisioned. I remembered Pop's words, "Every child has been born into the world with a message, a light clutched in his hand." There were many times when I didn't believe that God had given me a light or a message to bring to the world, times when I wondered where my life was going, and whether it would amount to anything meaningful. But He revealed my inner light, my special spark!

My friend, God is waiting for you to embrace chastity in your life! He wants to unleash your inner light! He wants to part the sea for you! And on the other side, you just might discover that your life — your mission — awaits!

You are the light of the world. A city set on a hill cannot be hid. Nor do men light a lamp and put it under a bushel, but on a stand, and it gives light to all in the house. Let your light so shine before men, that they may see your good works and give glory to your Father who is in heaven.

— MATTHEW 5:14-16

14

Your Mission

Before I formed you in the womb I knew you,
and before you were born I consecrated you;
I appointed you a prophet to the nations.
   Then I said, "Ah, Lord God! Behold, I do not know how
to speak, for I am only a youth." But the LORD said to me,
"Do not say, 'I am only a youth';
for to all to whom I send you you shall go,
and whatever I command you you shall speak.
Be not afraid of them,
for I am with you to deliver you,
                    says the Lord."

                                        — JEREMIAH 1:5-8

Prophets Empowered!
   The Bible is full of insecure prophets. Jeremiah had been chosen by God to be a prophet even before he was born. But when the Lord called Jeremiah to his mission, the young man resisted and doubted himself because he was so young. God reassured Jeremiah that He would give him the strength, courage, and understanding necessary for accomplishing the unique mission to which he was called.
   Jonah was similar to Jeremiah. God appointed him to call the people of the city of Nineveh to repentance. But Jonah felt like he wasn't up to such a big job, so he tried to run from God. He got on a ship to a faraway land, but God was aware of this and continued to pursue him! When Jonah finally answered God's call, he found that converting Nineveh was a lot easier than he

had expected. After only a day of preaching, the entire city repented! Even the king put on sackcloth and sat in ashes. With God's help, Jonah fulfilled his mission in just a day.

I can understand Jeremiah and Jonah (even though my mission is much smaller than theirs!). When God tapped me on the shoulder and asked me to speak about chastity, I frankly asked Him to find someone else! Like Jeremiah, I felt I was too young to speak out and not capable of bringing such a challenging message to the world. I tried to run from God's call, because I didn't think I had the courage or the ability to speak His truth. I was firmly attached to the routine of my life, working hard in school and planning out my future. But God's loving call, which began as a tiny tugging in my heart, became too powerful to be ignored.

Your Calling

Jeremiah and Jonah did incredible things. But you're called to do equally wonderful things. Like Jeremiah, you might sometimes feel that because you're young or inexperienced, you're not ready to reach out to others as a disciple of Christ. Like Jonah, you might think that you're not capable of doing what God asks, bringing your unique mission to the world. But God always believes in you, even in those times when you don't believe in yourself.

Just as God called me, so too does He lovingly call you to bring your special light to the world! He has given you a message and a mission that only you can accomplish. Your light shouldn't be hidden under a bushel basket but placed on a lampstand for all the world to see!

Going Deeper for Good!

At this moment, God's hand is upon you. He's asking you to be like the apostles, and to "put out into the deep and let down your nets for a catch" (Luke 5:4). Peter and the fishermen had been working hard, doing what they thought they were supposed to be doing, living out their routine, and leading normal lives in the eyes of the world. They never imagined what a wonderful plan God had in store for them!

God spoke to them through a frustrating situation. At that moment, they weren't accomplishing their goal — they weren't catching fish. But they were touched by Jesus' powerful message in His teaching. So when Jesus told them to go out into deeper water for a catch, Peter said, "Master, we toiled all night and took nothing! But at your word I will let down the nets" (Luke 5:5). In this simple act of faith, Peter and his friends opened themselves to God's will. Doing so, they hauled in such a load of fish that the boat almost sank and their nets strained to the breaking point! This was the beginning of their incredible journey as disciples of Jesus Christ.

When I won Miss Wisconsin, my heart was so full of joy that I literally felt like I was going to burst. That was almost more happiness than I could bear. My net was so full that it stretched to the breaking point! This was also a great step forward in my mission, more than I ever could have imagined.

Are you ready for the joy and inner peace, the freedom and challenge that will come into your life when you open yourself fully to God? You will live more intensely in each moment! Your life will take on new and greater meaning! You'll feel that, at last, you've come home!

Don't get me wrong — it's hard work. Just as it was tough for Peter and James to lift those heavy nets into the boat, it's tough to be God's disciple in the world today. You will face temptation, ridicule, and discouragement on your journey. But truly, that is minor compared to the fulfillment and happiness you will experience!

At this moment, Jesus is tapping on your shoulder. He's asking you not to settle for a watered-down life or a lukewarm faith. He wants you to be *radical*. To be extreme. To be a rebel. To stand with courage.

Keeping Your Eyes on Jesus

It's hard to believe that God calls *us* to the amazing mission of doing His work — especially when we look at ourselves, with all of our flaws and shortcomings. And when we look around us at all the obstacles and temptations that fill our lives, it sometimes feels impossible to follow God!

The trick is to keep your eyes on Jesus. Peter discovered this firsthand. When the apostles were in their boat, a great storm came upon them, and they saw someone approaching, walking on the water.

> They were terrified, saying, "It is a ghost!" And they cried out for fear.
>
> — MATTHEW 14:26

Actually, it was Jesus!

> But immediately he spoke to them, saying, "Take heart, it is I; have no fear."
>
> And Peter answered him, "Lord, if it is you, bid me come to you on the water." He said, "Come." So Peter got out of the boat and walked on the water and came to Jesus.
>
> — MATTHEW 14:27-29

Peter did — he was actually walking on the water! He was completely focused on reaching our Lord. But then he became frightened. The howling wind, the tumultuous waves, and his amazed friends distracted him. He took his eyes off Jesus and started to sink. He cried out, and Jesus reached out and saved him from drowning in the stormy sea.

Sometimes when we face difficult choices, we can take our eyes off of Jesus. Like Peter, we can be distracted by the adversity around us and forget that God's will is what will make us happiest.

Your Choices

The first important step to opening our lives to the greatest possibilities is to live God's will through our choices. My life would be a lot different today if I hadn't made the commitment to chastity. I would be a much different person! My friend, God's plan for you is so extraordinary, it's impossible for you to imagine! Just as it was impossible for Peter, a simple fisherman, to foresee that he would become the first Pope.

God speaks to you through every choice that you make. The pressures that you face each day, from popularity and academics, to sex and drugs, to any issue you can think of — these choices are important. They're opportunities for you to grow in God's love and to bring light to the world. One of life's most rewarding experiences is to be able to look at yourself in the mirror and know that you're a person of integrity — that you're someone who stands strong and does the right thing, and that you live your life based on the truth, without regrets.

But even more beautiful is to know that you're doing these things not only for yourself and for your future, but for God! To live your life well is a beautiful thing. Contrary to what society tells us, this is the most fulfilling and joyful way to live. Remember that Jesus didn't come to make us miserable, but to give us *joy!* "I came that they might have life, and have it abundantly" (John 10:10).

The beauty is that no matter what we're doing, however minor it might seem, Jesus shows us that this is a task through which we can glorify God. Whether you're running a race or studying for an exam, you can do it for Christ. Offer it to Him as a way to glorify His name and to thank Him for the many blessings of your life. We are abundantly blessed with gifts: faith, family, friends, food, shelter, talents, intelligence, the opportunity to go to school or pursue a career, and God's tremendous love and sacrifice on the Cross. All of these are worthy of our praise and thanksgiving! And we can offer these to Him every moment of the day by dedicating our lives and actions to Him.

What is your vocation? What is your mission? God speaks to us through the events of our lives. Just as He used the experiences of close friends to awaken me to my mission, so He is speaking to your heart. Perhaps He is calling you to be a teacher or a doctor or a priest. Perhaps you're called to be a social worker, a contemplative religious, a politician, or a stay-at-home parent. Perhaps He wants you to volunteer at a homeless shelter or mentor a child or form a prayer group on campus. God has entrusted to you a unique light, a *mission* to accomplish in the world.

My friend, at this moment, I challenge you *to open your life to this personal mission, by yielding to God's radical love!* Whatever your calling is, one thing is certain: God calls you to a life of chastity. By now, as you've journeyed with me through my story of making the commitment to chastity and speaking out for others, you must know that your sexuality is a beautiful gift! You also must know that *chastity is truly a call to real love!* And by journeying with the Lord through this book, I hope that you know that God loves you unconditionally!

God's hand is upon you now, at this special moment. He will be with you through every moment of your life, carrying you through those difficult times like the man in the "Footprints" story. He is longing for you. He is standing with His arms open, saying, "Come home." Don't keep Him waiting any longer.

As you put down this book and continue on your life's journey, I hope that you remember this journey that we have taken together. I hope that you never fear "casting out into deeper waters." I hope you never hesitate to take a leap of faith for Jesus. I hope that you always remember that you have a special, unique mission, an inner light to bring to the world. Your life is too precious, too important to be lived in a lukewarm or mediocre way. This is *your* wake-up call! Go deeper! Get out of the boat and walk! God has an *awesome* plan for your life! Don't settle for anything less, because it's the very best — a life based on truth and meaning, a life of love, a life lived to the fullest!

Your mission is waiting!

God, thank You for being with me throughout this special journey. I know that Your hand is upon me at this moment. You've given me a beautiful invitation — to live out chastity, regardless of my past choices or what my future holds. I say "yes" to You, O Lord! I welcome the awesome future that You have in store for me. I'm "casting into deeper waters"! I'm getting out of the boat and walking! I'm keeping my eyes focused on You, because "The only applause that I seek is the applause of nail-scarred hands."

Lord, I don't know what the future holds for me: There will be victories and failures, joys and disappointments. Help me to see the low times as preparations for success. Help me to stay strong and to always know that You love me and have a plan for me. Part the sea, O Lord. Unleash my inner light. With Your help, I will keep my eyes always on You — and live my life Standing With Courage.

About the Author

Mary-Louise Kurey grew up in Brookfield, Wisconsin, and graduated *summa cum laude* from the University of Wisconsin-Eau Claire, where she received her Bachelor of Music degree in voice with an honors diploma and was the commencement speaker for the Class of 1996. In 1998, she completed her Master of Music degree at Duquesne University.

In June 1999, Mary-Louise was the first contestant to win the title of Miss Wisconsin with the platform of "sexual abstinence until marriage." In spite of advice from "pageant insiders" that this platform would cripple her in pageant competition, Mary-Louise went on to become a Top Ten semifinalist at the Miss America Pageant, where she also won the talent competition with her performance of the Italian aria "Il Bacio," meaning "The Kiss."

Affectionately — and irreverently! — dubbed by her fans as "The Apostle of Abstinence," Mary-Louise spoke to over a hundred thousand teens and young adults across the country during her year as Miss Wisconsin. She continues to touch the hearts of thousands of young people at youth conferences, rallies, schools, camps, and churches all over the United States.

Her upbeat, high-energy message has drawn interest from print and broadcast media around the world. Through a wide variety of television, radio, and print-media interviews and coverage, Mary-Louise's message has reached over twenty-five million people on five continents. She makes regular appearances on *Politically Incorrect with Bill Maher* and *Life on the Rock*, in addition to appearing on many other radio and television programs, including *Janet Parshall's America*, *Kresta in the Afternoon*, *Church and Culture Today*, *Life and Choice*, and *Builders of Hope*.

From *The New York Times* — *London Edition* to *WORLD Magazine,* from Capitol Hill to Franciscan University, Mary-Louise is known for inspiring young people to make positive choices and achieve their dreams.

Mary-Louise was designated a national spokesperson and role model speaker for the national Best Friends character development program by its founder and president, Elayne Bennett. She received the "Character-in-Action Role Model for Youth — Friendship Award" from the organization for her service, inspiring participants to postpone sexual activity, reject drugs and alcohol, and strive for the highest educational, career, and personal goals.

Mary-Louise's dynamic message, inspiring personal commitment, heartfelt sincerity, and moving story have generated an enormous response throughout the nation.

To find out more about Mary-Louise's work, view photos of her "in action," or for more information on bringing her to your area to speak to teens and young adults, check out her website at www.mary-louise.com. She always enjoys hearing feedback about her book, answering questions, and coordinating online chats with teens and young adults interested in living out chastity. Log on — she'd love to hear from you!

Notes

Notes

Notes

Notes

Notes

Our Sunday Visitor. . .
Your Source for Discovering
the Riches of the Catholic Faith

Our Sunday Visitor has an extensive line of materials for young children, teens, and adults. Our books, Bibles, booklets, CD-ROMs, audios, and videos are available in bookstores worldwide.

To receive a FREE full-line catalog or for more information, call **Our Sunday Visitor** at **1-800-348-2440**. Or write, **Our Sunday Visitor** / 200 Noll Plaza / Huntington, IN 46750.

- -

Please send me: ___A catalog

Please send me materials on:

___Apologetics and catechetics   ___Reference works

___Prayer books   ___Heritage and the saints

___The family   ___The parish

Name_____

Address_____Apt._____

City_____State_____Zip_____

Telephone (   ) _____

A23BBABP

- -

Please send a friend: ___A catalog

Please send a friend materials on:

___Apologetics and catechetics   ___Reference works

___Prayer books   ___Heritage and the saints

___The family   ___The parish

Name_____

Address_____Apt._____

City_____State_____Zip_____

Telephone (   ) _____

A23BBABP

- -

Our Sunday Visitor
200 Noll Plaza
Huntington, IN 46750
Toll free: 1-800-348-2440
E-mail: osvbooks@osv.com
Website: www.osv.com